WITHDRAWN

THE
OUTDOOR
BOOK

Stonehenge: an oblique air view of the famous prehistoric monument in Wiltshire, once a double circle of dressed stones, with a double horse-shoe of stones inside the circle, all surrounded by a bank and ditch. Inside the bank is a circle of 56 pits, some of which can be seen here marked in white. A trek across Salisbury Plain to Stonehenge is first-class experience for young people who have been well briefed (Aero Films Ltd.).

THE
OUTDOOR BOOK

by

JACK COX

*Lightweight Camping · Youth Hostelling · Hill Walking
Fell Scrambling · Exploring by Cycle · Boating and Canoeing
Animal Watching · Bird Watching · Plaster Casting · Pond Life Study
Stream and River Study · Butterflies and Moths · Insects
Flowers, Plants and Trees · Outdoor Collecting Hobbies · Seashore Fun
Photography · Brass Rubbing · Painting and Sketching · Archaeology
Geology · Map Making · Conservation · Field Studies
Outdoor Recreation · Field Trips · Expeditions*

LUTTERWORTH PRESS · LONDON

First published 1954
Second Impression 1955
Third Impression 1957
Fourth Impression 1960
Fifth Impression 1963

Revised Edition 1970

ISBN 0 7188 1752 4

Printed in Great Britain
by Latimer Trend & Co Ltd Plymouth

Acknowledgments

In this book I have drawn largely on my own experience of practical field work with young people over many years, but since all successful outdoor expeditions depend on team work I have been deeply grateful to friends who have generously placed their own specialized experience at my disposal to show the wide and diversified range of activities now available to intelligent and enthusiastic groups of young people. This is acknowledged in the text where necessary.

I have been especially grateful for the facilities placed at my disposal at various times by the Duke of Edinburgh's Award Scheme, the Council for the Promotion of Field Studies, the Nature Conservancy, the Royal Society for the Protection of Birds, the Youth Hostels Association, the Scout and Guide Associations, the Institute of Archaeology at London University, the Council for British Archaeology, the Haslemere Educational Museum, the Royal Geographical Society and the National Federation of Young Farmers' Clubs.

Thanks are also due to the owners of copyright for permission to use photos as necessary, to Messrs. Seeley, Service and Co. Ltd. for permission to reproduce a specimen page of *The Bird-Watchers' Field Pocket-Book* and to Winston Megoran for his drawing of a dinghy with equipment reproduced on page 68.

Preface

THIS book is a handbook of practical ideas on a wide variety of outdoor hobbies and interests. It is intended mainly for teachers and youth leaders of all kinds who want to do some practical work outdoors with young people. Many youngsters may well read it themselves and find it of some value in their own immediate circle of friends, as they go exploring at week-ends and in the holidays, in twos and threes or small parties, on foot and on wheel, along the fair green ways of Britain. Theirs is the joy of real achievement.

I have not attempted to lay down hard and fast rules for tackling any one outdoor hobby or interest. The British temperament is not very well suited to accepting hard and fast rules, unless it has to do so in time of emergency. We prefer to find our own way once we have been given a lead, like all true individualists, and we are a nation of individualists. So this book tries to give a lead. It offers suggestions and ideas of proved value over a long period of time. There is nothing theoretical in its approach, for instance. The idea has been to select a number of outdoor hobbies and interests of special value to young people, for one reason or another, and then to show ways and means of getting on with the jobs which have been successful in practice.

Above all, it is a book of *ideas*. I do not use the word "should" if I really mean "can". I do not lay down "famous last words" and say that this or that is the way some activity or other should be approached, or accomplished. What I do say is something like this. Here is one good idea which has been tried out in the field with young people and found successful. This is the way it was tackled. You may prefer to adapt that method to your own particular youth group, whatever it may be, bearing in mind that we are dealing at all times with adolescents who are probably at varying stages of mental adjustment and physical development.

The way the reader tackles the ideas developed in this book, then, is not my concern. I make the suggestion and show how the practical work has been carried out by a variety of youth groups in differing parts of Britain. In this respect the book is a gathering of practical experience over a wide field, and over a period of years.

*   *   *

I have divided the book into four main sections with a number of chapters in each section.

In the first section (A) the aim is to show the reader the *method* of tackling a practical outdoor hobby or interest. These methods have not been chosen haphazard. They have proved to be excellent methods of carrying out work in the field. The instruction does not delve into excessive detail, but gives all that has been found necessary with a variety of youth groups.

The methods recommended are:

  i. Lightweight Camping
 ii. Youth Hostelling
iii. Climbing of a simple character, including Fell Scrambling
 iv. Exploring by Cycle
  v. Exploring by water, including boating and canoeing

*   *   *

Once these techniques have been mastered thoroughly by the teacher or youth leader, and his or her group of young people, it is time to consider what to do. A group which is starting from scratch may well spend its first year mastering the technique of the particular outdoor method in which it is interested, for example, lightweight camping and youth hostelling or fell scrambling. Some outdoor work can be done as well, but a great amount of time cannot be given to such work until the technique comes naturally and without effort, no matter what the terrain or weather might be.

Master, then, the technique and the method or methods chosen, and do not be satisfied with anything but the best. A slipshod camper or lazy youth hosteller is not likely to be a first-class bird watcher. Quiet, effective and efficient outdoor technique is not difficult to achieve. Once young people appreciate that lightweight camping, fell scrambling, exploring by water and so on are means to ends they will quickly master them and, what is more important, go on improving their technique with time.

*   *   *

I have graded outdoor possibilities into three main sections, again based on long experience. (These are sections B, C and D.)

In section (B) I discuss in general "What to Do" and suggest that a group can try Animal Watching, Bird Watching, Plaster Casting, Pond Life Study and Stream Life Study—in that order. All these interests are of a wide, general character.

In the third section (C) we pass on to more specialized interests, the study of Butterflies, Moths, and Insects, the study of Flowers and Plants and Trees, the amusing hobbies of "collecting" stiles, bridges, brasses of all kinds, old customs, folk-lore and so on, using camera and logbook.

The last and more advanced chapters are concerned with detailed field studies, and particularly Archaeology, Geology, Field Survey and Map Making. This can be fun, or heavy going, but it ought always to be fun!

All worthwhile outdoor work is also sport and recreation and if we approach it in that spirit we shall get a great deal of excitement and adventure from our outdoor hobbies and interests. What is more, we shall get a lot of useful field work done. This will be of infinitely more value to young people than the excessive intake of secondhand adventure and experience offered by mass media such as television.

I will be glad to hear from any leaders of expeditions who have found *The Outdoor Book* of value.

Contents

Contents

List of Plates

Line Illustrations

The line illustrations were especially drawn for this book by L. G. Goodwin with the exception of the Dinghy on page 68 which was made by Winston Megoran, and page 95, which is reproduced from A Bird-Watcher's Field Pocket-Book *by kind permission of Messrs. Seeley, Service & Co. Ltd., the author's maps on pages 186 and 190 and drawings on page 19.*

SECTION A

HOW TO GO ABOUT IT

CHAPTER 1

Lightweight Camping

LIGHTWEIGHT CAMPING enables a youth leader to carry out almost any kind of field study. It is particularly suitable for parties of boys on stream or river survey, or on a collecting expedition for botanical or geological specimens. Camping is truly a means to an end when lightweight camping is practised, and the whole kit is carried in a frame rucksack on the back. A reasonable standard of fitness and toughness must be expected, and with practice, over a season or two, it is surprising what high standards of camping can be achieved by young people.

Generally speaking, lightweight camping is best suited for teenage boys in relatively small parties, say, up to twelve or fifteen in number, under the supervision of an adult leader. Many girls, especially those who are experienced members of the Camping Club of Great Britain and Ireland, can trek well, using lightweight kit, and such activities as painting and sketching outdoors, or "collecting" stiles, bridges, old customs and so on may be well suited for them. But there are obvious physical limitations and the youth leader in charge of a party of teenage girls may find youth hostels, farms, or a standing tented camp (used as a base) more satisfactory. Mixed parties are a great success when based on youth hostels, but lightweight camping treks, in my experience, are best treated as a boys' effort.

No time should be lost in building up high standards of camping technique. The lightweight camper has probably had a good deal of experience in standing camps using heavy patrol tents, and about two or three seasons of such experience

B   17

is usually necessary before a camper is seasoned enough to try lightweight camping proper, in which the camping is merely incidental to the job in hand.

Let us therefore assume that a prospective party consists of one or two experienced adults and up to fifteen senior boys between the ages of 14½ and 18. The first essential is to split this party into small units of three, four or five boys using the patrol system which has proved itself so effective in practical Scout training. I have used three patrols of four boys in a trekking party with success, the party having two adult leaders. Each patrol of four boys had its own elected boy leader and assistant or "second".

The camping organization of such a trekking party is then based on this division into patrols of four, each with its own boy leader. Lightweight camping calls for relatively small, compact tents made of lightweight material (e.g. Egyptian cotton or nylon weave) and of a special pattern to accommodate one lightweight alloy or bamboo pole. The most suitable tents for our purpose are two- or three-man "hike" tents.

The tents that I have used most effectively on such treks are the Itisa Senior, now made in Protex by Messrs. Black & Edginton Ltd., who also make the famous Good Companions series. With such tents it was possible to use six lightweight tents to a party of twelve boys and two adults. Five of these tents were used for sleeping and personal kits (one for the leaders and four for boys, sleeping three boys to a tent). The sixth tent was used to store food and gear needed for the particular job in hand, e.g. plane table equipment for field survey practice. In a trek which is taking place in hilly or mountainous country the use of a sixth tent for this purpose can be dispensed with, since it is more essential then to consider loads, and the minimum tentage will be required. If the party has sound experience it can still be carried.

In general the use of a spare tent for food and gear is not a luxury. In wet or damp weather it is essential, while it makes for better and cleaner camping at all times, as well as ensuring that special equipment is not damaged.

As I am recommending patrols of four boys on lightweight

GOOD COMPANION

NEW TINKER JUNIOR

PAL-O-MINE

NEW ITISA SENIOR 69

ARCTIC GUINEA

NEW MOUNTAIN
(Blacks)

GILWELL JUNIOR

O.B. VENTURE 69

A selection of well-designed tents suitable for lightweight camping and mountain treks, and frequently used in Britain camping treks it is possible to use larger lightweight tents to sleep four boys so that a patrol is kept intact at all times. These larger models are of excellent quality but are not always technically suitable for use in exposed situations or on hill treks, where much of our field work is likely to be done. Alternatively, two-man hike tents can be used entirely, e.g. Gilwell two-man Hike Tents as sold by The Scout Shop, London. Allowing two such tents to a patrol a total of eight or nine would be required for a trek party of twelve boys and two adults.

The tentage problem will ultimately depend on finance! While it is desirable to equip a party with lightweight tents of sound quality and similar pattern the estimated cost involved may be beyond the resources of the youth group. In that case use will have to be made of a common pool of lightweight tents of varying pattern, weight, size and shape. There are many disadvantages to this system in practice, but not so many that a group should ever be discouraged from trying lightweight camping treks for that reason.

The great advantages of using tents of the same pattern, style and weight are:

1. The weights are at all times known and can be shared equally. This is important on a long trek.
2. In the case of damage (by wind, flood, snow, etc.) or loss (by theft or "act of God") individual tent parts can be interchanged, especially poles.
3. The area of each tent is known and a common system of sleeping and camping can be used.

The Camping Club has recommended a lightweight list which is accurate and based on long practical experience. It is entirely suitable for the average boy of sixteen and as a general guide can be used in the initial planning of a lightweight camping trek. The list is reproduced on the opposite page.

If essential personal items are added to this list the total weight carried can be kept down to 12 lb. per person or 14 lb. for one person. To this basic weight must be added that of food and gear carried.

The choice of food will test the initiative of any camper on

Weight for two *lb.*	*oz.*	*Equipment*	*Weight for one* *lb.*	*oz.*
4	7	Two-man Lightweight Tent	–	–
–	–	Standard Single-pole Tent	1	13
1	8	Metal Poles in Case	–	15
–	11	24 × 6 in. Metal Tent Pegs	–	–
–	–	10 × 7 in. Metal Tent Pegs	–	9
1	6½	Groundsheet, Lightweight	1	11½
3	14	Sleeping Bags, down	1	15
1	10	Pressure Stove for two	–	–
–	–	Pressure Stove for one	1	1
–	11¼	Cooking Canteen	–	7¼
–	6½	Mug(s)	–	3¼
–	6½	Plate(s)	–	3¼
–	3½	Knife, fork, spoon	–	1¾
–	6	1½ gallon Water Bucket	–	–
–	–	1 gallon Water Bucket	–	4¾
–	2½	Wash Basin (optional)	–	2½
3	15	Frame Rucksack	1	15½
–	8	Ground Blanket (optional)	–	11
–	3	Windscreen Pressure Stove	–	3
–	4½	1½ pt. Aluminium Milk Can	–	–
–	–	1 pt. Aluminium Milk Can	–	3½
–	12	3 Food Boxes	–	–
–	–	2 Food Boxes	–	8
–	½	Salt Box	–	½
–	2¾	Torch	–	2¾
21	10½	i.e. 10 lb. 13¼ ozs. each	13	3½

lightweight trek. One problem is that of obtaining fresh vegetables when in the hills far from farms and shops. I recommend particularly the "Swel" brand of dehydrated vegetables (mixed green vegetables, carrots, onions, swedes, beetroot) for this purpose. They are easy to prepare and the flavour is good. A wide range of prepared camp meals are now available at leading camping equipment shops and many grocers. Boxed or canned the only problem is carrying and storage until use.

Other very useful foods which I have tested under varying conditions include Tetley's tea bags, coffee (Nescafé, Maxwell House or H.A.G.), fruit and nut cake, chocolate, dried fruits, dates, packet cheeses of all kinds, Kendal mint cake, and the Swiss-made "Knorr" range of packet soups. I recommend the

clear beef bouillon also made by Knorr, Symington's dehydrated soups, concentrated skimmed milk powder (a 2 oz. tin
makes 2 pints), Bovril Pemmican (lean meat, beef fat and yeast
in 1 lb. tins), and several "instant potato" preparations for
making mashed potatoes. The most suitable sugar, if required,
is in the form of very hard "Pure Cane Coffee Sugar" crystals,
made by Manbré and Garton Ltd., London, W.6, and supplied
in stout 1 lb. containers. For bread supplies I have invariably
carried 1 lb. Hovis loaves, in linen bags, which will keep up
to a fortnight. Wholemeal loaves are, however, cheaper and
various crispbreads and rye biscuits are now widely used.

As the group gains experience the problems of food and gear
will become all-important. The art of successful lightweight
camping is what to take, and what to leave behind. In a trekking
party such as we have visualized there are many things that can
be shared, especially where personal and trek kit gear are concerned. These include toothpaste, soap, toilet paper, shaving
cream, torches, compasses, maps and food. One lightweight
camper can carry a prismatic compass while his companion
carries a torch; another can carry the group's First-Aid kit
while his companion carries the maps and so on. All this entails
a good deal of advance planning in detail. Such planning and
"staff work" is never boring. In fact it is always fun and adds
greatly to the success of the trek.

I am laying down no hard and fast rules on lightweight camping as practised for treks. Personal preferences vary greatly and
have to be considered. If a boy wants to carry a china mug and
plate to the ends of the earth in preference to aluminium or
enamel ones let him do so. He probably has good reasons. My
experience has been that basic weights *must* be worked out for
the entire party and shared equally. Any personal kit a boy
carries in addition to the agreed basic weight is his own responsibility entirely. One good trek of three, five, seven, ten or fourteen days will soon convince him of the essential nature of his
personal kit.

Effective use can be made at all times on a camping trek of
the *Poste Restante* system of the Post Office, under which clothing, food and equipment can be sent in parcels addressed to

Lightweight camping in the Alps near Zermatt; and (below) a well-sited camp in Hertfordshire, using lightweight equipment (D. W. Gardner).

Senior boys received instruction in archaeological field work at this fourth-century Romano-British site (Hal Morey).

oneself c/o the Postmaster of any Post Office on the proposed route, excepting town sub-offices (see the Post Office Guide). This is the best way to get a change of underclothing, and to ensure specialist food supplies in isolated areas. Why carry unnecessary loads if the Post Office will do the job effectively? This may outweigh the prevailing postal charges.

I have emphasized the use of a patrol system with elected boy leaders in units of fours. This enables the "buddy" system to be used when the trek is in progress, with the boys working in pairs at all times, each boy being responsible for his particular "buddy". This discourages boys from wandering off on their own in difficult or dangerous country (e.g. moorland, mountain, bog, etc.) and enables some sort of check to be kept on the party. The patrol leader is responsible for knowing where his own three boys are at any time. In practice one will be with him and the other two in the near vicinity. I stress the wide and effective use of the "buddy" system on camping treks. It makes for good discipline within the team as a whole, and without sound discipline of the voluntary kind the trek will not be a success at all. Lightweight camping treks do a great deal to build up character in the individual. While there is room for individual tastes and differing personal temperaments (and we are dealing with young people at an impressionable stage in their development as individuals in a free society) there is *not* room for temperament as a whole!

The kind of things which can ruin a lightweight camping trek with a purpose behind its camping are the usual human failings. It is useless, for instance, to allow lounging around cooking fires, or having strange meals at odd hours. It is equally useless to have the morning rouse and the evening lights-out at hours which might be in order for gentlemen of Bohemian habit on the London stage, but completely out of place in a job of work for intelligent young people. The discipline has to be there, and accepted or enforced voluntarily. Everest would never have been climbed without the kind of team discipline that we need to have in our own modest treks.[1] Without such voluntary

---

[1] For sheer inspiration read *The Ascent of Everest* by Sir John Hunt, published by Hodder & Stoughton.

discipline we shall get nowhere at all. It will come quite easily and naturally if the individuals have confidence in their adult (and boy) leaders, and in themselves. The leaders have a responsibility here in setting up standards of achievement and behaviour which will inspire young people in their charge. A good team spirit is not difficult to achieve and maintain with young people of guts, initiative and intelligence. The effort made to achieve it will be found really worthwhile.

*   *   *

Some further consideration can be given at this stage to the technique of lightweight camping.

I have not so far said anything about flysheets. Most lightweight campers use them when camping in "green" country or the hills. Their value *can* be overrated. Personally I like them, providing I am camping leisurely. I like to stick my shoes and cooking gear and things I do not really need outside the tent, under the flysheet eaves. Invariably that space soon becomes full! I am not, however, convinced entirely that flysheets are an enormous advantage in the British climate. Our sun is rarely hot enough to make camping uncomfortable without a flysheet, but it is often wet enough to make camping with one a more comforting business than it would otherwise be, although we do not get the heavy continuous tropical downpours that go through a lightweight tent as if it were made of muslin. We must always remember, too, that a flysheet practically doubles the cost of a tent, and good tents are not cheap.

As far as our trekking is concerned, always remembering that we are going to be on the move a good deal, flysheets can safely be left at home or dispensed with altogether. They are simply not necessary when we are carrying everything. A really good trekking team of sound experience can even camp without tents at all, using, instead, ground sheets above and below the body for sleeping, with a bivouac woodcraft or proofed canvas shelter over the head. The method has some obvious drawbacks, but it is worth trying sometime for the sheer fun of it. Hedgehogs are likely to be disconcerting at times, but in high summer it can be excellent training for experienced campers.

GROOVE

TENT

LONG-HANDLED
DUAL-PURPOSE
TROWEL

WATER
BUCKET
WEDGE-TYPE

GROUND
PLATES

BULLDOG
PEG

LIGHT AXE
1½ lbs.

HUNTING
KNIVES
(TWO IN ONE
SHEATH)

TOILET HOLD-ALL
AND TENT WALL POCKET

SKI
HAVERSACK
FOR
HOSTELLING

WATER
STERILIZING
TABLETS

GILWELL
CANTEEN

WATERPROOF
SLEEPING
SHELTER

PLASTIC
BUTTER
BOX

KNIFE,
FORK AND
SPOON SET IN
STAINLESS STEEL

BERGAN
RUCKSACK

TENT
LIGHT

POCKET PETROL STOVE

HIGH PACK
EVEREST
RUCKSACK

FOLDING
WINDSHIELD
FOR PRESSURE STOVE

*A selection of the most useful items of modern lightweight camping
kit and equipment used by experienced campers and hostellers on trek*

As far as possible sites can be arranged in advance in the usual way on lightweight camping treks. If all the party or group are members of, say, the Camping Club or the Scout or Guide Associations this will present no difficulty, and the Camping Club site list is invaluable. But if sites have to be found, let us find them as early in the day as possible to make certain we have permission to camp on the chosen site. It is simply not worth it to "take a chance". Lightweight campers who do so run the risk of letting all other serious campers down, and putting a good site out of bounds for all time to campers. *The standard of Lightweight Camping is the code of Good Camping, which cannot be too high.* If you have any doubt about this at all consult the Camping Club handbooks and Lord Baden-Powell's *Scouting for Boys*. It is assumed in this book that camping standards are already high before lightweight trek camping is even contemplated. Lightweight camping, indeed, is not for the novices. It is a magnificent sport, and the full value of it, and the fields it opens up to the camper of imagination and resource, cannot be experienced by the novice or "greenhorn".

*   *   *

In general, cooking on trek is best done by pressure stove. A supply of "Metaldehyde" (solid methylated spirit in tablet form) can be carried for starting the stove (and a windshield of some kind is advised) but the use of paraffin can present problems. I have tried with success the method of "caching" supplies of paraffin and canned food in advance of a trek at set points, particularly in hilly and mountainous areas. I know it represents an artificial aid to trekking in some ways, but all successful expeditions set up bases and supply points, and I see no reason to condemn the method. We cannot employ teams of sherpas and porters to carry our supplies and gear, however attractive the prospect might be!

The leader should know the country in which he is taking a trekking party, and if he sees it in advance from a car seat while "caching" stores at suitable supply points he can always convince himself that he is doing a preliminary reconnaissance in style. (After all, the successful Everest team practised in North Wales and the Alps.)

Another alternative is to pin-point garages on the One-inch O.S. map and to send runners for paraffin when needed. We can always use woodfires and dispense with pressure stoves if we wish. It usually is not possible in the hills, however. *The success of the trek depends not on whether we cook by woodcraft fire or modern pressure stove but on what we do on the trek.* In other words, real "camping with a purpose." Does it matter how we cook our food so long as we get a hot meal on time with the minimum of effort and labour? We are already experienced campers and not in danger of losing our woodcraft knowledge and lore if we happen to use pressure stoves. Nor should we neglect petrol "hike" stoves of the kind used in Sweden. They need care in using and handling *en route*, but campers of real experience speak very highly of them.

I would also emphasize these further points because they were consistently important in all lightweight treks in which I have taken part:

1. A light alloy entrenching tool, or garden trowel with 18-in. handle, is essential for the simple shallow overnight latrine. A screen of some kind is necessary in hilly country but can be dispensed with in "green" woodland camping country.
2. Waterproof match boxes are *essential*, and spare torch batteries and bulbs.
3. Odd lengths of waterproof silk, or a few oiled silk tobacco pouches, can be extremely useful in many ways.
4. A selection of ball-point pens of good quality with varying colours of ink can be most useful for noting field information direct on to black-and-white Six-inch maps.
5. Daily foot inspections must not be missed. All trek campers can get in the habit of carrying foot talc powder and using it daily. Blisters can ruin lightweight camping treks. Therefore we avoid them.
6. Keep a list of doctors, hospitals and First-Aid points in the area. They may never be required in twenty years of trek camping. They may be needed on the first trek we undertake.

7. A sensible First-Aid kit can be carried by each patrol. It need only be small so long as it contains the essentials.
8. If we wear wool we will be comfortable and happy on trek in spring, autumn and winter! This is a fact, not a fad.
9. A can or bottle of neat's-foot oil is worth carrying by one member of the party. Its daily use on shoes or boots is good for morale as well as keeping the leather in trim. On a hot and dusty July day this point can be appreciated.
10. We take out an insurance policy to cover our camp gear and equipment against loss by theft. This is not the advice of a pessimist, or cynic. It is a precaution we shall feel glad we undertook if it should unfortunately be necessary to make a claim.
11. We do not attempt too much in any one day! It is easy for teenage boys to overdo things in the enthusiasm of the moment. The leader can only learn by experience when his team has had enough.

*   *   *

Above all, lightweight trekking is fun, and that includes the object of the trek, even if it is as deadly serious as archaeology or geology.

If it is not fun something is certainly wrong. It may be our own approach to the whole thing.

FURTHER READING

Scouting for Boys—Lord Baden-Powell (Pearson/Hamlyn)
Camping and Woodcraft—Horace Kephart (Macmillan)
Camping for All—Jack Cox (Ward Lock)
Camping Club Handbook and Site List, issued to members of the Camping Club of Great Britain & Ireland Ltd.,
    11 Lower Grosvenor Place, London, S.W.1.
Camp and Trek—Jack Cox (Lutterworth Press)
Modern Camping—Jack Cox (Stanley Paul)
Lightweight Camping—Jack Cox (Lutterworth Press)

CHAPTER 2

Youth Hostelling

YOUTH HOSTELLING is a first-class method of carrying out practical field work with young people, and particularly for mixed parties. In fact there is simply no better way for the teacher or youth leader with a group of teenage boys and girls interested in some basic field study such as botany, geology, field survey, geographical studies of land forms, social and local history, village life and rural arts and crafts. I have carried out, for instance, compass traverses in Dovedale with groups of teenage boys and girls based on Hartington Youth Hostel, as well as plane table surveys in the area around that particular hostel, which is well sited for the purpose.

The object of the excellent Youth Hostels Association is quite clear. It exists "to help all, especially young people of limited means, to a greater knowledge, love and care of the country-side, particularly by providing hostels or other simple accommodation for them in their travels, and thus to promote their health, rest and education". Recognizing the invaluable nature of such work, the Department of Education and Science has made large grants towards the purchase of youth hostels. The great advantage over lightweight camping is, of course, the relative cheapness.

A lightweight camp kit can only be built up at a considerable capital cost. Seen in its right perspective this is comparatively cheap, since it will give so many years of first-class service (a three-man hike tent of my own, made of lightweight Egyptian cotton, was still usable after twenty years of hard service). Venture Scouts, particularly seem to like lightweight camping treks and there is the splendid work achieved by the British Schools Exploring Society every year.

But youth hostelling is a positive solution to the problem of "how to go about it" if the initial capital cost of lightweight camping kit cannot be overcome. The wise youth leader will try both methods, and possibly use both consistently. Some activities that can only be carried out on a lightweight camping kit are not suitable for work based on a youth hostel trek.

My experience has been that lightweight camping is ideal for real, continuous trekking and all activities where a party of boys, especially, are walking or cycling in the country-side, camping overnight at some pre-selected site. Youth hostelling is especially suited for a mixed group of young people carrying out field work in a definite area and based on a youth hostel, to which they return each evening.

Where only two or three young people are carrying out work on their own, such as gathering specimens of wild flowers or plants, or photographing or sketching old bridges and unusual stiles, then youth hostelling becomes a tramping trek with a variety of hostels used, each night if necessary, in the same way as overnight camps using lightweight kit on a camping trek.

Some 200 youth hostels in England and Wales are able to accommodate School Journey Parties. The students need not necessarily be Y.H.A. members, although they are encouraged to join after their first hostelling trip. Youth hostels offer the opportunity, at low cost, to lead a simple community life in clean and pleasant surroundings. With the increased attention now given to field studies and outdoor educational projects, many schools arrange for hostel visits to take place during term time as a normal part of the curriculum. Full details of the facilities available are given in a booklet, *Youth Hostels for School Journey Parties*, from Y.H.A. National Office, Trevelyan House, St. Albans, Hertfordshire.

For more advanced field studies, the Y.H.A. has equipped 20 hostels, in specially selected areas, with workrooms and apparatus for use by school parties. The all-in charge at these hostels for students and teachers is 18s. per head per day (1969–70). A booklet *Youth Hostels for Field Studies* gives details.

Teachers and youth leaders who wish to introduce youngsters to hostelling as a leisure activity, outside the school curriculum, may make use of the Y.H.A.'s Leader Card Scheme. This enables a maximum of fifteen youngsters under 21 to be taken hostelling for not more than three nights, without becoming Y.H.A. members.

*   *   *

In general, youth hostelling parties must be accompanied by adult leaders in the ratio of one leader of the same sex for each 15 boys or girls. Each leader should be an experienced member of the Y.H.A. If the party is a mixed one then there must be an adult leader of each sex in the party. Additional leaders need not necessarily be teachers, but they should be members of the Y.H.A. Normally leaders sleep in the same dormitories as the boys or girls in their charge.

The maximum stay permitted in any one youth hostel is three consecutive nights. This may be extended in the case of a School Journey Party carrying out a special task, such as a plane table survey in the area around the hostel. A trek involving the use of several hostels can easily be achieved by a youth group of some hostelling experience. Since most hostels are well used at weekends, particularly in the spring and summer, the youth leader will be wise to concentrate on mid-week projects in term time, thus avoiding weekend holiday walkers and the peak summer holiday months of July and August.

My experience has been that the Y.H.A. could not be more helpful to mid-week parties of young people carrying out field work under adult supervision. The wardens in general are especially helpful, and the National Office of the Y.H.A. at St. Albans will gladly give any youth leader contemplating such a trip the benefit of its wide experience.

Most school or youth club parties will require the all-in service of the hostels. At the time of writing the charges are: 6s. a night for those aged 21 and over, 5s. for those aged 16 and under 21, 4s. for those under 16. A three-course evening meal costs 4s., packed lunch 2s. and breakfast 3s. Each member of the party must use a sheet sleeping-bag of the approved Y.H.A. type. They can be hired at all hostels or bought at 15s. each.

It is important to realize that youth hostels are for those who travel on foot, or by cycle, or canoe. They *cannot* be used by motorists or motor cyclists, or coach parties, although coaches may be used to enable a party to reach a selected area in which hostels exist.

Among the areas specially recommended for young people because of existing hostel facilities are the Weald, the North and South Downs, the New Forest, Dartmoor, Exmoor, the Quantocks, the Devon and Cornish coasts, the Cotswolds, the Forest of Dean, East Anglia, the Brecon Beacons and the Black Mountains, the coast of Pembrokeshire, the Longmynd, North Wales and Snowdonia, the Peak District, the Yorkshire Dales, Upper Teesdale, the North Yorkshire moors and coastline, the Roman Wall and the Lake District. These largely cover the National Parks scheme, but the areas named are specially suited for a wide variety of field studies based on botanical, geological and geographical themes.

Hostelling is ideal for the mixed party which intends to explore historical market towns or cathedral cities, and the recommended list includes Bath, Cambridge, Canterbury, Chepstow, Chester, Colchester, Exeter, Lichfield, Lincoln, London (especially Roman London), Ludlow, Norwich, Oxford, Plymouth, Saffron Walden, Salisbury, Shrewsbury, Stratford-on-Avon, Street (for Glastonbury), Winchester, and York. There is enough exploring for young people in these fine towns and cities to keep them occupied for years.

Suggestions put forward by the enterprising Y.H.A. include simple exploring treks in the border country between Shropshire and Wales. Both history and geology offer rich sources of ideas for both lightweight camping and youth hostelling treks in this area. In the Eastern Counties a ten-day cycling tour can cover a number of fine hostels and enable a group to explore some of England's finest colleges, castles, cathedrals, churches and great country houses. If this does not appeal it is a classic area for geologists and botanists and artists. There is a valuable series of *Regional Booklets* published by the Y.H.A. at modest prices which give ideas and useful information to any youth leader.

The Y.H.A. no longer has direct links with farms but it does include visits to farms and forestry plantations in the Countryside courses.

Hostelling in Ireland

Youth hostelling in Ireland is still relatively in its infancy; there were 16 hostels in Northern Ireland in 1969 and about 7,000 members in the Y.H.A. of Northern Ireland Ltd., while the Irish Youth Hostel Association, known widely as An Oige, had over 8,000 members and operated an additional 41 hostels. Very few parties of young people go to Ireland to take part in planned field trips and outdoor treks using youth hostels as bases, but there is obviously wide scope for enthusiastic, well-led parties from all parts of England, Wales and Scotland.

The difficulty in planning any Irish treks centres round the close association of Irish youth hostels with the official Irish tourist industry and the fact that the hostels are full of young holiday-makers, many from the Continent, the Commonwealth and the U.S.A., in the popular summer months of July and August. But if these peak holiday periods can be avoided then Ireland has a very great deal to offer with its magnificent scenery and opportunities for outdoor projects and expeditions of all kinds, particularly in the fields of geology, geography, archaeology and pre-history, bird- and animal-watching, botany, sailing, boating and angling, as well as sketching, painting and photography.

Travel arrangements by air or sea, with connections by train or road, are now easy, and party rates reduce the cost considerably. In Northern Ireland pre-booking, as it is called, is essential for all parties and groups at Easter, Whitsun or any other time, and full requirements must be stated at this provisional stage. Applications should be made by responsible leaders or individuals direct by post to The Organizing Secretary, Y.H.A. of Northern Ireland Ltd., 28 Bedford Street, Belfast 2.

C

The 16 hostels in Northern Ireland are fully equipped, with mains water supply and modern sanitary arrangements; no prepared, hot evening meals are provided as in hostels in England and Wales, for instance, but there are ample cooking facilities by gas, or meals are usually available within easy reach elsewhere. Each hosteller needs to take his or her own cutlery, tea towels, and sheet sleeping bags as well as the normal personal kit, but sheet bags can be hired at modest fees if required. Hostel charges for 1969 onwards are 2s. 6d. per night for all below the age of 16, and 5s. per night for all aged 16 or over. There is one exception to this scale at the Ballygully hostel where the fees are 3s. 6d. per night for all below the age of 16, and 6s. per night for those aged 16 or over.

The Y.H.A. of Northern Ireland Ltd., often called Y.H.A.N.I. now, publish an attractive handbook at 1s. 3d., plus postage, which contains much useful information on Irish place-names as well as a whole range of practical suggestions for hostel tours in the North of Ireland. The advice on local weather conditions is particularly valuable and it needs to be followed closely in conditions of mist in mountain and moorland areas. Hostellers are urged to carry a compass at all times when the weather is cloudy. The distances between hostels are given and there are detailed routes for cycling and walking tours.

Recent hostelling treks in Northern Ireland of an experimental nature have included such projects as a survey of the Ben Crom reservoir in the Mourne Mountains, and a geological survey of the attractive coastline of Antrim and Derry, including the famous Giant's Causeway. Other hostellers have preferred to explore the high and trackless moors of Antrim. There is a folk museum on the Scandinavian pattern at Cultra and another small but good museum at Stranmillis. The Sperrin Mountains, the Mountains of Mourne and the Fermanagh Lake District are all within easy reach of Belfast and well worth exploring with the help of youth hostels. Near Waterfoot there are some raised-beach caves in the Triassic sandstone which will provide useful survey material for geographers and geologists. Bird-watchers can visit Fair Head and watch many varieties of gulls and other sea birds swooping hundreds of feet below them. Murlough Bay is another haunt for bird-watchers.

A most useful and attractive map of Northern Ireland is published by the Northern Ireland Tourist Board and is available free on application to the Board at 10 Royal Avenue, Belfast 1. In addition to all the essentials it marks and lists accommodation, camping sites, hostels, restaurants and cafés, National Trust properties, and all the Ancient Monuments in Northern Ireland, both those in State care and those in private hands, a most useful guide.

There are as yet (1970) no organized outdoor activities using the 41 hostels of An Oige in the Irish Republic, but the opportunities are there in abundance for the seeking. None of these hostels may be used between 10.30 a.m. and 5 p.m., which for some leaders may be a disadvantage at times, but full and up-to-date details may be had by writing to The Manager, Irish Youth Hostel Association (An Oige), 39 Mountjoy Square South, Dublin 1. All applications for hostel bookings should be made to the same address. The overnight fees are 4s. per night for "seniors and juniors" and 2s. 6d. "for juveniles under 16"; in Cork and Dublin hostels these fees are increased to 5s. for "seniors and juniors" and 3s. for "juveniles under 16". There is a special fee for groups of 2s. 6d. per night, including leaders, which is increased to 3s. for Cork and Dublin hostels. There are few restrictions in Irish hostels, but it is important to note that the use of transistors and portable radios is not allowed at any time.

The link between the Irish tourist industry and An Oige is a close one, as it is in Northern Ireland, and groups may find it easier to plan a holiday trek or one that combines some field work with sightseeing rather than a continuous programme of active outdoor projects. Three publications of real value are the official Handbook of An Oige which is obtainable by post from the address given above at 2s., plus postage, and two publications for which there are no charges; these are the brochures *Holidays and Weekends in An Oige Hostel* and the *Guide to Ireland's Hostels and Places of General Interest*. Both contain a great deal of practical information.

One term used frequently in Irish youth hostel literature is "a drum-up", but this means simply "an outdoor meal" of almost any kind. An Oige says, tersely, that "rain capes are essential at all times" and although this need not be taken too literally it is a reminder that no one can go to Ireland without some kind of outer garment for wet days. The most useful seem to be the waterproof anoraks now sold in so many attractive and colourful styles, or the very useful, all-embracing capes for outdoor use sold by Black and Edgington Ltd. mainly for use in Scotland, Wales and the Lake District, but equally good for Irish mountains and moors.

All hostellers in Ireland are urged to carry map, compass, torch and first-aid kit at all times and to stay put at once if a sudden mist descends. Six An Oige hostels are exceptionally well-sited for mountain walking and climbing, and eleven more are convenient centres for bathing, all forms of sea fishing and the study of marine life. Six more hostels have been specially sited to provide bases for freshwater angling and coarse fishing. The handbook provides many proved suggestions for 7 and 14 day tours which can be adapted by any leader to his or her own work on outdoor projects.

One recent field survey of the coastline of Donegal by a small party of Midlands students all under 19 combined camping with youth hostelling; they discovered that five hostels in Donegal were ideally placed for their purpose. Much use was made on this trek of inexpensive hired boats with local fishermen as guides. The trek was undertaken in early to mid-April and the weather conditions were good enough for camping without special precautions other than a substantial diet. There never seems to be any shortage of this in any part of Ireland at any time of the year.

The An Oige Handbook contains a valuable reading list of 30 books on Ireland but some which are specially recommended by recent trekkers include:

The Islands of Ireland—Mason (Batsford, 1950)
The Caves of Ireland—J. C. Coleman (The Kerryman Ltd., 1965)
In Search of Ireland—H. V. Morton (Methuen, 1938, New Edition 1964)

The Mountains of Ireland—D. C. C. Pochin Mould (Batsford, 1955)
The Forests of Ireland—(Society of Irish Foresters, 1966)
Prehistoric and Early Christian Ireland, Estyn Evans (Batsford, 1966)
The National Monuments of Ireland—(Bord Failte, 1965)
Walking in Wicklow—J. B. Malone (Helicon Press, 1964)

*   *   *

Although this book is concerned mainly with practical outdoor and field work in Britain it is worthwhile to emphasize the international character of youth hostelling. An enthusiastic youth group which decides to concentrate on youth hostelling as its chosen "means to an end" will sooner or later want to go abroad, just as the enthusiastic lightweight campers will. Full information about the International Youth Hostel Federation is readily available, and can be had from Y.H.A. Sales and Services at 29 John Adam Street, London, W.C.2. The International Youth hostel handbook, containing details of all hostels on the Continent, costs 6s. 2d., post free, from the same address.

The Y.H.A. itself arranges continental walking and cycling tours, as well as less strenuous sightseeing holidays, all with an experienced Y.H.A. leader. Tours abroad are also arranged for teachers and youth leaders wishing to lead their own parties. Winter ski-ing parties are arranged, too. All this gives the youth leader some idea of what is available to his youth group and to what extent exploring treks can develop.

In Britain, the Y.H.A. organizes a popular series of *Adventure Holidays* for those aged 16 and over, with activities which include walking, cycling, pony trekking, sailing, canoeing, photography, bird-watching, archaeology, brass rubbing, caving, mountaincraft, countryside discovery, gliding, painting and sketching, orienteering, rural crafts and diving. For boys and girls aged 11 to 15, Eagle Adventure Holidays provide a slightly more limited range of one-week activities. These holidays, under the guidance of an experienced Y.H.A. leader, are all suitable for beginners.

Brochures of *Holidays Abroad*, *Winter Sports Holidays*, *Adventure Holidays* and *Eagle Adventure Holidays* may be obtained from Y.H.A. National Office (address on previous page).

*　　　*　　　*

Hostellers of long experience say that the most important asset to the young hosteller is the ability to accept the spirit and purpose behind the Y.H.A. Unselfishness is the outstanding personal characteristic in the good hosteller and that is very important to a party such as we visualize of twelve to twenty boys and girls carrying out practical field work under adult supervision.

The same patrol and "buddy" system can be used as in light-weight camping treks and the same general principles of organization in the party can be followed. More field work can be tackled and a more ambitious programme followed, simply because the party is not carrying tents, food and incidentals like sleeping bags and cooking gear. (Field survey is especially suited to youth hostel bases for this reason, since its equipment can be bulky.)

A code of hostel etiquette needs to be drawn up by the youth leader and rigidly observed. It would include:

1. Nailed walking shoes or boots *must* not be worn in the hostel itself. A pair of light plimsolls, sandals or soft shoes should be carried to wear in the hostel.
2. The risk of fire must at all times require special precautions, especially if the accommodation is in barns, converted farm buildings and so on. Some hostels are historic beamed buildings of great age. A few still use oil lamps for lighting. The leader in charge of a youth party needs to take every possible precaution against fire while his party is using a hostel.
3. Close co-operation with the warden will ensure smooth working at all times. It may be inconvenient to a leader to get his or her party out of the hostel by 10 a.m., but there is a very good reason for it.
4. The accepted hostel chores such as washing-up, bed-making,

cleaning, etc., must be undertaken by a youth group as if they were ordinary youth hostel members.

5. Elementary precautions such as the padlocking of bicycles together if the party is a cycling party are the responsibility of the youth leader in charge of the party. A warden cannot be held responsible for theft of property while a youth group is staying at his hostel.

6. It helps if stamps or s.a.e's are always enclosed for replies when making advance arrangements by post with a youth hostel warden.

7. It is not necessary to separate lightweight camping and youth hostelling completely where trekking is concerned. At some hostels members of the Y.H.A. can bring lightweight tents and camp in the grounds of the hostel on payment of 2s. to 3s. per person. This enables hostels and tents to be used in field work in an area where they may not be many hostels.

Lastly, the Y.H.A. has a reputation for giving courteous and accurate information to those who seek its help. The youth leader who cannot find his or her own immediate problem answered in Y.H.A. literature should not hesitate to write to the National Office, giving full details of what he has in mind and where he wants to go with his School Journey Party or Youth Club. A solution will surely be found. If photos are taken of a youth group at work while based on a youth hostel the Y.H.A. would always appreciate spare prints. They are useful in giving leads to other youth groups.

FURTHER READING

The Hike Book—Jack Cox (Lutterworth Press)
Camp and Trek—Jack Cox (Lutterworth Press)
The Youth Hosteller—published monthly by The Youth Hostels Association, Trevelyan House, St. Albans, Hertfordshire. (Annual subscription 8s. 6d.)

The Y.H.A. publish an annual *Adventure Programme* for which no charge is made and which lists the special-interest hostelling holidays of the year arranged by the Association. The

1969 edition, for instance, included details of hostel treks arranged for canoeing, aqua-lung diving, painting and sketching, sailing, gliding, caving, walking, pony trekking, photography, archaeology, cycling, orienteering, brass rubbing and ornithology. The cost of such hostel trekking holidays varied between £8 10s. and £20 per week, with an average price of £12 to £15 for most special-interest weeks.

Once an area has been chosen for a youth hostel trek suitable books on the topography of the area may be borrowed from Public or County lending libraries.

CHAPTER 3

Hill Walking and Fell Scrambling

ONCE we have mastered the simple technique and "feel" of good lightweight camping and youth hostelling with relatively small youth groups based on patrol organization, we can tackle hill walking and climbing, fell scrambling and even mountain treks. The latter is not impossible if we use plenty of common sense, surely the most useful asset in any kind of outdoor work with young people.

In this chapter I suggest a few useful main thoughts to keep in mind when on the hills with young people, whether at home or abroad. There are many delectable areas to choose from for hill walking in Britain, including the Lake District, Snowdonia and Scotland. The Lake District is specially recommended, as it is a splendid choice for any number of tramps or youth hostel treks. It is also such a good area for outdoor work, being compact, easy to reach by train, coach or car, and well served for youth hostels and farms catering for the needs of hill walkers. It has a magic appeal of its own which makes it ideal for novices and all new to fell scrambling and hill walking, as well as to old hands. The area is unusually rich in both animal and bird life.

Let us first think about climbing as far as young people are concerned, bearing in mind the physical limitations and lack of experience of our prospective party or group.

Really experienced climbers of all grades, and in Britain they are mainly rock climbers, emphasize the need to pay special attention to weather conditions. The determining factor in all hill work is, indeed, the weather. A youth leader may well

spend some considerable time discussing local weather conditions and probabilities with local outdoor people who know
what they are talking about. Gamekeepers, wardens, verderers,
telephone linesmen, farmers and farm workers as well as surveyors, golf professionals, groundsmen of football clubs, bus
drivers, quarrymen, geography masters in local schools, and
even milk roundsmen—all have given me valuable local
weather tips at varying times. I emphasize this to all youth
leaders—learn and absorb local weather lore from local people,
especially those who have lived in an area all their lives.

Once this rule has been established we can get down to detail
planning and policy. Although we call for the use of common
sense at all times, and caution when necessary, we are not going
to take the spark of adventure right out of everything we do.
Reasonable risks have to be taken, but we need not be foolish
or foolhardy. We need to know, too, the limitations of our own
particular party so that we can decide, almost instinctively after
a time, what is within our capacities and what is beyond us. We
shall not always be right. If we were there would be no fun in
hill trekking and fell scrambling at all.

One very experienced climber, who led many parties of
young people in the hills, emphasized:

1. There's no disgrace in giving up and turning back.
2. Never tackle anything beyond one's experience or strength.
3. Don't take a single step further up unless one is *sure* one
   can get down.

I know no better or simpler code for the type of work we
have in mind. It is also significant that both adults and young
people who get into trouble on the tops, and find they are in
the position of a famous, if mythical, goat which could neither
get up nor down, are always foolhardy.

Conquer hills before mountains, in the true Everest tradition.
The trekking party of young people which has absorbed the
feel of green hills and heathered slopes in all kinds of weather,
and knows something about way-finding in misty conditions
on the same slopes, is achieving something.

Young people should not wear climbing boots that are too

heavy for them, nor should their boots, or shoes, be too heavily nailed. It is a common fault. Not only does a heavily-nailed boot tire youngsters more easily, but also in cold weather the metal rapidly conducts heat away from the feet. Cold feet at Easter is more often due to over-generous nailing than anything else.

It would be easy to give much advice at this stage on anoraks, balaclavas and so on. But we are dealing with individuals. Their temperaments and personal requirements in the way of clothing vary like the fell breeze itself. Work out your own needs with your own group. Common sense is the only worthwhile measure. Common sense demands that young people on hill treks should be warm and well fed at all times.

From my own experience I have found that five or six small meals in a day are better when hill trekking than three large ones. The gaps between breakfast and lunch, and supper and breakfast, are vulnerable points with young people. The routine food intake may well be: hot breakfast at farm or hostel; mid-morning small meal of chocolate biscuits, dates, dried fruit, hot drink; sandwich lunch with fresh fruit and hot drink; afternoon small meal of rich fruit cake or raisin chocolate; hot meal in evening about 7 p.m.; hot drink and biscuits before sleeping. This may seem enormous at first sight. On a cold, raw day in early spring or autumn it may seem painfully inadequate. A constant supply of dried fruit, raisins, raisin chocolate, and dates is necessary to keep up body heat and energy. A few parcels to replenish "stock" can be posted to oneself at any Post Office on or near the trekking route.

It is hard to impress on young people that the shortest distance between two points on the hills is not necessarily a straight line. If they insist that it is then let them scramble a little in scree and bog and stream valley. The mosquitoes in the Lake District in June, July and August may prove a better teacher than the adult in charge of the party.

Steep hill slopes in the Lakes and Snowdonia have to be tackled on occasion and then we can use the well-tried zigzag approach, taking our time, and preferring heather to bracken —if we have the choice. If in time real climbing is undertaken then proper practice under adult supervision is at all times necessary. The technique of teaching by experienced climbers involves the constant practice of foot- and hand-holds on suitable terrain and exposed rock faces or outcrops where the youngsters may only be two or three feet off the ground. Until an adult youth leader has seen this training in practice he, or she, will scarcely believe that so much technique can be mastered under such simple conditions. A mountain does not have to be high, and remote, and forbidding, to be difficult and dangerous. Climbers of real experience have graded one of the Harrison Rocks, known as "The Niblick", near Tunbridge Wells in Kent, as very severe, yet it is only forty feet high.

A youth leader may well take his exploring party on trek through limestone country in the Peak District, or the Cheddar Gorge, or along the Chalk Downs. It is a temptation to youngsters to try and scramble up the nearest cliff faces. Their soft and crumbling nature makes them dangerous, or at least completely unsuitable for such activities. Fortunately such areas are well served with "Danger" notices. Treat *all* such notices with the respect they deserve.

If sudden mist on the hills envelops the party we put into operation our own emergency hill code. North Wales is notorious for sudden mist, by the way, and Scotland is not far behind. The pleasant hills around Llangollen, for instance, can be deadly dangerous when mist swirls round. If there is a wind at all at any time note its prevailing direction. That will be useful knowledge when mist is dispersing. A series of compass bearings can be taken and noted on prominent landmarks, if any. Positions can be fixed or pin-pointed constantly on the One-inch O.S. map. *Don't go on any further if at any time the mist is thickening.* Instead, retrace the original track taken, using map and compass, and return with caution, always providing the terrain is known.

If visibility is practically nil, and the party is really caught on the tops (it happens to all of us at times) stay put and do not wander. Keep the party intact, make for the nearest stone wall —an angle of walls is ideal under such circumstances—and make the party as comfortable as possible, putting on every available woollen garment! The dates, biscuits and chocolate will really be useful then, as well as sing-songs. Use whistles if necessary and keep listening for other parties' signals. The accepted SOS whistle code in Britain is six blows each minute at ten-second intervals followed by a minute's silence. If it has to be used make it continuous by using all available people in relay.

Each party will naturally prefer to select its own trekking area, and for varying reasons and projects, but the following suggestions have proved most successful with young people. The notes can be greatly amplified and added to by consulting my companion volume *The Hike Book* (Lutterworth Press):

1. *Salisbury Plain*. Rolling downland with wood and valleys. Easy country; good for beginners and short treks in spring and early summer.

2. *Welsh Borders*. More exciting but similar country in many ways. The classic Offa's Dyke (Prestatyn to the Severn) is difficult to follow in parts but well worth the effort of tracing it; probably best at its northern end, since it can so easily be reached from large centres of population.

3. *Brecon Beacons*. Good everywhere and first-class in spring. Be ready for more trees than you imagined which requires sound map-reading. A particularly fine area for compass traverses and much achievement in a short space of time, which appeals to young people in the early stages.

4. *Cheviots, Galloway Hills, Bowland Fells, Exmoor, Dartmoor, and the Yorkshire Dales* (*especially Wharfedale*). Superb trekking country and open moorland. Can be quite strenuous and is best tackled in the spring and early summer for that reason. Wharfedale particularly recommended.

5. *The Peak District*. A bit of everything and wonderful training ground for all walkers from Edale to Dovedale. Too stark for some people but the bleaker moorlands can be avoided easily. My favourite is Dovedale with Hartington Hall youth hostel as base; no better terrain for compass traverses and self-contained treks exists.

6. *The Pennine Way*. This magnificent 250-mile path was the

first long-distance route under the National Parks footpath scheme. Between 1950 and 1969 no less than 1,500 miles of footpaths and bridleways had been established or designated in Britain, 1,200 miles by the National Parks Commission alone in some of Britain's finest scenic areas. In 1969 the Pennine Way was still the only one with a right of way throughout its 250-mile length. A proposed linking path to the Lake District will extend it by a further 50 miles; Edale–Northumberland–the Lakes will then be a reality. Two books published in 1968 provide much detailed advice; they are *A Guide to the Pennine Way* by C. J. Wright and *The Peak and Pennines* (also for use with No. 5 route) by W. A. Poucher; both are published by Constable.

The historian A. J. P. Taylor, a well-known walker who believes that walking is an ideal way to show how landscape has moulded history and influenced it, walked 100 miles of the Pennine Way in June/July 1968 with his son. They made a rendezvous with a car at set points each day so that they could find accommodation in more hospitable valleys. This method has also been used with school journey parties in North Wales, where lorries have taken parties each evening to hostels or houses converted into field activity centres (e.g. the Hertfordshire County education authority).

7. *The Yorkshire Coast and North York Moors Path.* A relatively new route of 93 miles within easy reach of large areas of population. Particularly recommended to bird-watchers and botanists.

8. *The South Downs Way.* A straight trek from Beachy Head to Winchester and Salisbury. There are many variations of route to suit the individual but in all there are some 80 miles of trekking that is more strenuous than seems possible.

9. *The Pembrokeshire Coast Path.* This is a magnificent trek of 167 miles in all with undulating and pleasant coastline offering scenic beauty, many bird-watching projects and accessible beaches. I followed much of this path in April, 1968, and was surprised at the variety of terrain in short stretches of only 15 to 20 miles.

10. *The Ridgeway Walk.* Brian Dunning has aptly described

this 200-mile route in these terms: "among gourmets of the British landscape the Ridgeway will probably rank as the most elegant of the cross-country paths."

The route starts properly at Cambridge and then skirts the northern ridge of the Chilterns, through Bedfordshire and Hertfordshire to Wallingford. Then across Berkshire and Wiltshire via Avebury, the Vale of Pewsey, Warminster, to Cerne Abbas in Dorset and finally in a great spurt to the Channel coast at Seaton Bay, Devon. By 1968 the central part of this old and traditional route, some 68 miles in fact, had been surveyed and mapped and soon the entire 200 miles will be covered. The Ridgeway is the historic route used for carrying flints from the mines at Grimes Graves, near Thetford in Norfolk, to Avebury and Stonehenge.

11. *The Chilterns.* So near to London and yet so neglected! For a sample of the Chiltern flavour a party or group or section can take a fast train from Marylebone, stopping at Harrow-on-the-Hill and Moor Park, then each station on the Aylesbury line, to Wendover. The steep chalk ridge starts almost at the station and soon one is right on top with really magnificent views of the Vale of Aylesbury and far beyond.

It is a 20-mile trek of absorbing interest to the fine old Oxfordshire village of Nettlebed via Chinnor and Christmas Common. Nettlebed is on the Oxford–London South Midland coach route via Henley-on-Thames and this will take one to Victoria coach station or earlier points like Chiswick. Bookings should be made in advance. (See plate opposite page 160 for a Chilterns logbook page.)

The Chilterns are an important part of The Ridgeway Walk and their lovely beech woods are one of the outstanding features of the British landscape at all seasons, even in the depth of winter. An alternative to Nettlebed village as a terminal point on the route mentioned is to proceed via Christmas Common to Turville Heath, Stonor and the Assendons to pick up the London coach at Henley-on-Thames. In this area one of the exciting new proposed paths is a Thames path for walkers starting at Kew and linking up with the Ridgeway Walk near Goring and Streatley.

12. *Brecon Beacons to Bangor, North Wales*. This could be a natural follow-up to route No. 3, but it is a strenuous and tough project and the participants need to be fit. Get out the maps and work on the route yourself; it is too trying for high summer and is best done in the spring. On this route it is possible to walk as long as 32 miles without crossing a single road, which is saying something for a country like Britain which has the highest density of road traffic in the world!

13. *Sea Walks*. I have experimented with many of these over the years. The new footpath which is to follow the whole of the Cornish Peninsula may well be exciting to many, but I have personally been disappointed in Cornish walking, probably through doing it in summer months when we were hampered by persistent sea mists. More satisfying were short treks at the western end of the Isle of Wight ("the Freshwater weekend") and some fine June jaunts in the Isle of Man concentrating on the west and north of the island, from Peel to the Point of Ayre and Ramsey to Snaefell. The Lleyn Peninsula in North Wales was not a serious challenge but Bardsey Island is well worth the effort of crossing to by boat; the fierce unceasing breezes of the Lleyn Peninsula take some getting used to and make map work a little difficult.

14. *Island Treks*. My list is not exhaustive by any means but two of the finest are Anglesey (which may well become one of the longer, if not long-distance, paths) and Skye. To walk right round the island of Anglesey (including as much of Holy Island as one can) with lightweight camping kit, following the coastline as far as possible, is exhilarating. As a student, mapping the changing coastline of the island, I did it both ways with Rhosneigr as my starting and finishing point, and found the difference in approach quite startling. If an outdoor enthusiast ever walks round an island then he or she must do it both ways to get the proper effect. Anglesey, which ought to be a National Park, offers some of the finest bird-watching in Britain, as well as botany, wildlife, butterflies and moths, archaeology and pre-history *ad lib.*, geology, exceptional seashore study, sailing and boating, castles and forts.

I have repeated Anglesey treks many, many times with young

people from Lancashire, Yorkshire, Cheshire, the Midlands and London; I have never known such treks to be a disappointment, even in bad weather or a summer as dry and difficult as 1959. Newborough Warren and Llandwyn Island form a self-contained area for exploring.

Skye is magnificent, with everything in abundance. My choice, based on a 1964 reconnaissance in detail, is Duirnish, the western part of the island which is almost an island in its own right, with Dunvegan as base. There are excellent camp sites at the head of Loch Dunvegan; bird-watching with the study of gannets and buzzards in particular, animal-watching (seals, especially); loch fishing from boats, long moorland and cliff-path walks, botany and history (Dunvegan Castle of high renown), pony trekking, which is well done with parties as large as 30 sometimes, and the Skye Games at Portree for a splendid day's outing, make it a memorable summer trek.

The tougher stuff is not that far to the South in the Cuillins, where the mountaineer can find everything he wants. My approach, after an overnight sleeper from London to Inverness, was down the Great Glen to Kyle of Lochalsh, and then by a little steamer to Portree, followed by 24 miles by road in a school bus to Dunvegan for good measure. But the more likely alternative now is one of the ferries, Kyle of Lochalsh/Kyleakin or Mallaig/Armadale, with a bus or coach to connect. The journey to Skye is long (about 26 hours from London) and expensive, but once there no one will ever say it was not worthwhile. Further details and more schemes for the Hebrides will be found in my book *Lightweight Camping*, which is the most recent of the series I started with *The Outdoor Book*, the others being *Camp and Trek* and *The Hike Book*. Another feature of Duirnish is a beautiful white beach which will enable any collector of shells to have a field day. The trek to Vaternish for the site of old historic clan battles is also a highlight.

15. *The Tanat Valley, North-Central Wales*. I have often recommended this beautiful valley for self-contained treks for mixed parties. There is a great variety of undulating terrain, with shaded broad stretches of a tinkling river much loved by

D

anglers, and leading up to wild country with reservoirs and many moorland and heath birds. The Tanat can be approached from Oswestry with the best stretches leading from Llangedwyn onwards up into the delightful Berwyns. The Tanat valley can be linked with other youth group activities: for instance, the International Eisteddfod at Llangollen in July, where the rich offering of folk-song, dance and festival from all parts of the world is astonishing in its cultural standards.

These are nothing more than suggestions and I have offered nothing to those who ask for Irish treks where my experience is still far too limited. One cannot do everything but Northern Ireland and many parts of the West and South-West coasts offer much.

Other paths contemplated by the National Parks Commission may well be a reality before the next impression or edition of this book is prepared. They include paths of a gentler nature, with obvious attractions to the artist and collector, the photographer, botanist and so on. There are, for instance, paths following the Basingstoke Canal and the Kennet and Avon canals; also a path linking the Coniston Old Railway southwards and the disused railway track of the Pickering to Goathland railway line in North Yorkshire. More positive use is proposed of the Cotswolds which suffer too much from "day trippers", in the nicest sense, from London and Oxford. The fine old honey-stone villages of the Cotswolds are worth more than an excuse for a drive out of Oxford and a meal in some ancient inn. A route that combines a visit to some of the more interesting colleges of Oxford and an afternoon of a good cricket match at the famous Parks, and then a steady week walking in the Cotswolds, ending with a morning or afternoon in Gloucester Cathedral, is only one possibility.

A footpath is also proposed in the Shropshire hills, and an intriguing regional path in the Wolds of East Yorkshire, from the Ampleforth valley to the Humber. Meanwhile many county authorities are pressing energetically ahead with new plans. Hampshire County Council proposes "to extend the walkable section of the Pilgrim's Way from Farnham to Winchester", while Cheshire County Council proposes a 28-mile path round the Wirral, incorporating a disused railway line, the towpath of the Shropshire Union canal and existing rights of way.

The Northern Ireland National Trust opened the Antrim Coast Path, "the most spectacular cliff walk in Britain", in 1966. Not far behind in initiative is the Scottish National Trust which wants a long-distance path following the Roman Dere Street into England. The suggestion is a 70-mile path from Inveresk through Lauderdale to the Border, which could then link with the Pennine Way. I cannot do better than quote Brian Dunning: ". . . we are moving into an age of mass leisure; an age in which the majority of people expect, and get, official amenities, guidance and protection. To some the planned official footpath is anathema; but to others it is better than no footpath at all."

*   *   *

Essential points to consider for hill trekking include:

1. Study the area to be trekked on every available map in varying scales, e.g. One-inch, O.S. and Quarter-inch Bartholomew, or the 1/50,000 scale O.S. if available.

2. Relate any special object of the trek (e.g. botany, geology, geography, archaeology, bird-watching, etc.) to a planned route on the map. Stick to it, and don't deviate.

3. Set a daily mileage task and keep to it. Don't overdo it. The first three or four days can have short "legs" when we are getting into trim. From then onwards for the ten or fourteen days we can be full out. A daily average of eight to twelve miles, depending on the party and the object of the trek, is usually possible. Boys can do up to fifteen miles a day: ten is a fair average. Everything depends on whether lightweight camping kit is being carried, or youth hostels and/or farms are being used.

4. If youth hostels are being used advance booking is absolutely essential.

5. Wear sensible clothes at all times and keep strictly to the Country-side Code. Good manners are as essential in the country as anywhere else.

6. Rely implicitly on the advice of reliable and experienced people who live in the area and know it intimately. They are rarely wrong; we may often be.

FURTHER READING

Map Reading for the Countrygoer (Ramblers' Association)

Climbing in Britain—J. E. Q. Barford (Pelican Books)

Cross Country—Theo Lang (Hodder & Stoughton)

Scottish Hill Tracks—D. G. Moir (Albyn Press, Edinburgh)

Hill Walking in Snowdonia — E. G. Rowland (Camping & Open Air Press)

Snowdonia: The National Park of North Wales—F. J. North, Bruce Campbell and Richenda Scott (Collins)

The Yorkshire Dales—Marie Hartley and Joan Ingilby (Dent)

The Regional Books series, or Portrait series, published by Robert Hale Ltd., especially *Pembrokeshire* by R. M. Lockley and *Portrait of the Cotswolds* by Edith Brill

The Mountaineer's Week-end Book—Showell Styles (Seeley, Service & Co. Ltd.)

Getting to Know Mountains—Showell Styles and Jack Cox (Newnes). Cadet limp cover edition also available.

Regional Booklets of the Y.H.A., full details of which may be had by writing to Trevelyan House, St. Albans, Hertfordshire.

Four 1968 titles in the Constable's Pocket Guides series; all are profusely illustrated and written by W. A. Porcher: *The Scottish Peaks, The Lakeland Peaks, The Welsh Peaks* and *The Peak and Pennines*.

A Guide to the Pennine Way, 1968—C. J. Wright (Constable)

A Regional Guide to the Birds of Scotland, 1968—Kenneth Richmond (Constable)

CHAPTER 4

Exploring by Cycle

EXPLORING BY BICYCLE, either alone, or in twos and threes or in the company of other experienced cyclists, is a most pleasant way of knowing the country-side. In a single day's ride a cyclist can cover anything from ten to a hundred miles—even more if he is fit. A bicycle can be taken almost anywhere, in fact anywhere where a boy or girl can walk. In practice only an expanse of water or a sheer cliff face can really stop a bicycle, even though there are ingenious ways of overcoming both obstacles!

Some cyclists are content so long as they are in the fresh air; others like to add a spice of adventure by touring along green lanes, up moorland tracks and over mountain passes; while bird-watchers, amateur historians and amateur archaeologists find bicycles a useful means of transport at all times. Cycling is not hard work if one rides correctly. Long distances can be covered without fatigue provided that food is available as soon as one begins to feel hungry; but time should be allowed for wandering round castles, cathedrals and prehistoric sites. Chats with local inhabitants—postmen, fishermen or castle wardens —delay the cycle explorer, but it is time well spent, for people, as well as scenery, give a district its own special character.

No one really ought to set out on a long cycling holiday until he or she has gained experience near home. It is a good idea to join a local cycling club. Even if the explorer does not ride regularly with the club he learns a great deal about cycling from more experienced members. In any case, the more young people cycle the easier it becomes, so make use of every opportunity to go cycling.

The choice of a bicycle is of utmost importance. Naturally,

the first consideration is comfort, and this can only be achieved if the frame is not too large and the saddle and handlebar can be adjusted to give a good position. An expert, like Ronald English, recommends the "club" type of machine for cycle exploring. Its lightness is an advantage when climbing stiles or scrambling over rocks where it is necessary to carry the machine. Also, the lighter the machine, the less energy used when cycling. The dropped handlebars enable the explorer to use all the muscles in his body when climbing hills or riding against head-winds, and the fittings are designed to permit adjustments and repairs to be carried out with the minimum loss of time. The cyclist who prefers flat or upturned handlebars will choose a "lightweight tourist", or a "club" mount fitted with flat bars and a broader saddle.

Good position and style are the result of experiment and practice; but the following points may be taken as a guide by the average cyclist. Adjust the saddle so that one foot can touch the ground without dismounting. When cycling the knee should be slightly bent at the lowest point of the pedal. Move the saddle back until the peak is about 3 in. behind the bottom bracket. Fix the handlebar so that the top is level with the top of the saddle. With a "club" model a handlebar drop of 3 or 4 in. is plenty. Choose bars with grips at least 15 in. apart, and fairly broad at the top so that the cyclist can ride comfortably with the hands on top of the bars. Whatever the shape of the handlebar, the grips should point slightly downward towards the rear of the machine. A handlebar extension of $1\frac{1}{2}$ or 2 in. will suit most riders; but the length of extension required varies with the type of handlebar and the frame angles. The only satisfactory way of finding the correct extension is to borrow two or three and try them.

If the position is correct the cyclist will lean forward sufficiently to throw part of his weight on to the front wheel. The distribution of weight between handlebar, saddle and pedals is essential both for easy cycling and for maintaining proper control over the machine. With the arms slightly bent, and not over-stretched in order to reach the grips, the explorer can pull on the bars when climbing hills without swaying backward and

forward as so many inexperienced cyclists do. All cycling authorities are agreed that the feet should turn the pedals, not simply
push them down and wait for them to come up again. The
pedal is thrust forward before it reaches the top, and as the
foot goes down it is straightened so that the pedal is "clawed"
round at the bottom. There is an art in "ankling" that can only
be acquired by constant practice.

Most beginners think that any variable gear is infinitely better
than a single gear. This is not necessarily true. A single gear of
the correct size is better than a variable gear having a middle
gear too high or too low for normal cycling. For normal riding
a gear of 66 in. suits the average cyclist. If a variable gear is
fitted the middle, or normal, should be about 66 in. The expert
cyclist with a single gear pedals, more or less, at the same speed
up hill and down. To do this he must use more energy when
climbing hills than he does on the level. The purpose of a
variable gear is to enable the rider to maintain the same rate of
pedalling without appreciably increasing his output of energy.
By engaging a lower gear the speed of the cycle is reduced
while the cyclist continues to pedal at the same rate. A bottom
gear of 56 and a top of 74 provide a wide enough range for
most parts of the British Isles. A medium-ratio three-speed hub
with a 46-tooth chainwheel and 18-tooth sprocket gives gears
of 57·6, 66·4 and 76·8, while the same three-speed hub with a
40-tooth chainwheel and 16-tooth sprocket gives 56·4, 65 and
sprockets having 21, 18 and 16 teeth gives gears of 56·9, 66·4
75·1. A derailleur gear with a 46-tooth chainwheel and
and 74·7 in. All the gears quoted are for a 26-in. wheel. Many
lightweight machines are fitted with 27-in. wheels and five-
speed derailleurs. In this case the recommended sprockets are
26-, 22-, 19-, 17- and 15-tooth, giving gears of 47·8 56·4, 65·4,
73·0, and 82·8 with a 46-tooth chainring. The beginner needs
to study a gear table and variable gear chart before making a
choice.

The hub gear is cleaner and better protected than the
derailleur; but is more difficult to repair, and the ratios cannot
be changed. If a smaller sprocket is fitted all the gears go up
correspondingly. With the derailleur type most repairs can be

carried out by the wayside, and the ratios can be altered simply by fitting one or more different sprockets. Although derailleur gears are most popular with club cyclists the advantages and disadvantages of both are about equal.

We cannot expect a bicycle to be used regularly without giving occasional trouble; but much inconvenience can be avoided by proper maintenance. *At least once each year* the explorer's machine needs to be dismantled, the bearings and working parts examined and cleaned, and badly-worn bearings or fittings replaced. A weekly maintenance routine when brakes and bearings are checked and oil applied where necessary will keep the machine in running order. In addition a very thorough check is needed before going on tour, when gears may be lowered to suit more hilly country than usual or to allow for the extra weight of camping equipment, and tyres can be renewed or replaced by heavier ones for the rough tracks that will certainly be followed, if real exploring is to be done.

Wheels, pedals and bottom bracket axle must turn freely without any side-play. Adjustment in all cases is simply a matter of slackening a lock-nut or lock-ring, turning a cone or ball-cup, and re-tightening the lock-nut. The bearings need oiling every 200 to 300 miles, heavy oil being used for the hubs, bottom bracket and head bearings, light oil in the pedals, and thin, non-clogging oil in free-wheels and three-speed hubs. The oil should be injected through the nipples provided for the purpose. When the bearings (except those in a free-wheel or three-speed hub) are being assembled after overhauling they can be packed in thick grease. The best way to deal with a chain is to brush it in a paraffin bath, dry it, then dip it in thick grease that has been thinned by warming. Surplus grease can be wiped off before re-fitting the chain. It is important that every drop of paraffin is removed before applying the grease.

When oiling a free-wheel, lay the machine on its side and spin the wheel as the oil is injected. If the free-wheel is sticking or is dirty, flush it out with paraffin before applying the oil. A three-speed hub can be flushed out with paraffin from time to time, always followed by a good dose of thin oil. The brake levers, cable and brake arms need oiling, too, and the frame and other metal parts cleaned with oil. Care must be taken to exclude oil from the linings of hub brakes and from the rims where brake blocks are intended to grip. Always have the brake blocks adjusted to within $\frac{1}{8}$ in. of the rim.

Every keen cyclist, no matter how interesting his own locality may be, sooner or later wishes to explore other districts necessitating a tour of several days or even weeks. Many beginners have doubts about finding accommodation, and they book bed-and-breakfast for each night in advance. Part of the freedom of a tour is lost if one has to keep to a fixed route, and it is seldom necessary to book accommodation, except in the height of the summer season. Even in the holiday season few of the recognized cyclists' resthouses are full until 6 p.m. or 7 p.m., and sometimes much later.

The best plan is to start looking out for a suitable "bed-and-breakfast" place in the afternoon, say about tea-time. The cyclist can then wash, have a good meal, and explore the town or village.

The Cyclists' Touring Club and British Cycling Federation each produces its own handbook containing addresses and details of places providing accommodation for cyclists. These range from small farm-houses to moderate-sized hotels, and the C.T.C. handbook has over 3,000 of these addresses. Each address has been recommended by one or more members of the organization. The cost of bed-and-breakfast ranges from 12s. 6d. to £1 10s. per night. The handbooks are sold to members of the associations, and the addresses of these organizations are: Cyclists' Touring Club, Cotterell House, 69 Meadrow, Godalming, Surrey, and British Cycling Federation, 26 Park Crescent, London, W.1. Membership of the Cyclists' Touring Club includes the two-monthly magazine *Cycletouring*, which is the only British cycling publication devoted entirely to touring.

Today, a great many cyclists are using Youth Hostels on their tours. Hostelling is dealt with elsewhere in this book; but there is one point that the cyclist must bear in mind when planning a tour. In the holiday season and at weekends it is necessary to book accommodation at most hostels. To make the best of this restriction, choose hostels not too far apart and explore thoroughly the country between them. It is not necessary for the explorer to plan a route. He can go round in circles or figures of eight, and make detours to places of special interest without having to worry about accommodation. Early in the evening he can turn towards his next hostel and reach it in time for supper.

Undoubtedly, the cyclist with the greatest freedom is the one who carries his house with him! A single-pole lightweight tent of good quality, a lightweight oiled-fabric groundsheet, sleeping-bag, toilet equipment, shoe-cleaning material, cooking outfit and food are the chief requirements. Besides being free to cycle in any direction he pleases, there are no time restrictions on the explorer as there are at resthouses and hostels. Normally, he should select his camp-site with care and always obtain the permission of the farmer or landowner before using his land; but in the wilder parts of the country there is much open land where one can pitch a tent without disturbing anyone. As far as possible it is wisest to seek police advice before thinking of pitching a tent on open or common land. If the explorer wants to be cycling at the break of dawn there is nothing to stop him from striking camp at an early hour, provided he does not owe anything for the use of the site. Even then camp-site "dues" can be left in an envelope at the farm-house.

Most cycling campers keep cooking down to a minimum by buying a hot meal during the day and using a pressure stove for making tea and, perhaps, frying an egg or snack for supper or breakfast. Sufficient drinking water can be carried in feeding bottles, and a canvas bucket can be filled from a stream for washing. Two or more cyclists can share much of the camping kit, thus reducing the weight each must carry; but a lower set of gears than normal is advisable. A daily mileage of thirty or forty miles is plenty when loaded. In addition to the camping kit already mentioned an explorer will usually need pyjamas (a controversial point!), spare shirt, spare socks, pullover, eating utensils, a tin-opener and a first-aid outfit. A battery lamp or torch will be useful if the cycle is fitted with a dynamo outfit. A length of cord and a tent-peg can be used as a guy to keep the cycle upright. Drive the peg into the ground and tie the free end of the cord to the seat-pin, leaning the machine slightly away from the peg. Rain will do less harm to an upright mach- ine than one lying on its side. It should not be necessary to remind campers that litter left on the site or a fire lit without the farmer's permission may result in other cyclists being refused permission to camp.

Cyclists using resthouses or hostels can pack most of their kit into a fairly large touring-bag. When choosing a bag in- tended for holidays as well as weekends, select the largest and strongest. It is much better to have room to spare than to have insufficient room. It is possible to tour with no more than a cape, pyjamas, spare pair of socks, pullover, puncture-repair outfit and tools. If comfort in the evening is a consideration, pack a spare shirt, pair of trousers (gaberdine for preference) and walking-shoes, and still have plenty of room for maps, camera, books and other equipment. Each tour has its own packing problems created by the equipment to be carried. Some cyclists take a considerable amount of photographic equipment, others need binoculars for bird-watching or boxes filled with moss for preserving wild flowers, and so on. The touring-bag will need a support underneath to prevent it from bumping on the mudguard.

Some cyclists prefer panniers instead of the touring-bag attached to the saddle. Two panniers hold more than a touring- bag, and they keep the weight low down, making the machine more easy to handle. Campers may use one pannier for food, the other for clothing, and a touring-bag for toilet equipment and articles required during the day. The tent and sleeping-bag (wrapped in a groundsheet) are strapped on to the pannier carrier. Clips costing a few shillings are made for attaching portable pressure stoves to bicycle frames. One or two feeding bottles in a carrier on the handlebar will hold water or other drink, and, if the explorer is still short of room for his kit, there are small panniers that fit over the top tube at the front of the frame. To carry a pack of any sort on the back is uncom- fortable, unnecessary, and definitely dangerous.

No experienced cyclist would think of setting out for a day's ride without a reserve supply of food in his touring-bag. It may be dates, apples, biscuits or chocolate, anything that will keep a few days if necessary. Ordinary hunger can wait until the explorer reaches a café or finds a suitable place for a picnic; but "the knock" comes suddenly, and must be appeased straight away. Many a beginner has stopped cycling after a bout of "the knock", thinking that cycling is hard work, when all that he needed was a few dates or raisins. In remote parts of the country it is wise to pack a meal or two in the bag in case there are no shops when food is needed.

Clothing for cycling comes second to feeding. Shirts, shorts, ankle socks and cycling shoes are sufficient in hot weather. Ordinary shoes are too broad, too heavy, and too deep for comfortable cycling, and canvas shoes provide no support for the feet. A zip-fastener cycling jacket can be carried under the cape straps when not in use. A pullover and spare pair of socks should be packed even on a short run near home. If a cycle explorer does get wet feet or feels cold it can be dangerous to stand about without putting on warmer clothing. *In winter, follow the rule that it is better to be too warm than too cold.* Wear plus-fours, woollen underwear, a thick pullover and lumber type of jacket. Never wear tight clothing or shoes. A cape, sou'-wester and, possibly, a pair of leggings form the usual water-proof outfit. The cape should be fairly long, and at least 120 in. round the bottom. Leggings that cover only the front of the foot and leg are best. Always hang up the cape when not in use.

"Exploring by cycle" does not mean setting out on a ride without making preparations or plans. On the contrary, an explorer is most scientific with his preparations. For the runs near home get to know the country thoroughly from books on history and topography, museums and maps. Fixed routes are undesirable. The explorer sets out on his bicycle, looking at his map, and turns to the right or left down a lane for no other reason than that he feels like exploring it. He may know that the Saxons settled in the district, because he has read about them. He sees the marks of the old ridge and furrow cultivation practised by the Saxons in the fields beside the lane. A moat is marked on the map. He walks a few yards across a field to look at it. It probably belonged to a pre-Elizabethan manor house. Was the lane here when the first feudal lord built his manor? He can look for clues when cycling and search for more information in library books on winter evenings.

A knowledge of his own district will help the explorer to understand more distant districts that must be explored on holiday. He can decide where he is going to spend his Easter or summer holiday well in advance so that he has time to read a few books (including fiction) featuring the district. Get those maps early, too, so that they can be browsed over. For most areas the half-inch contoured maps are adequate; but the Ordnance Survey One-inch maps are best, and are essential for following mountain tracks and exploring areas covered with prehistoric sites. Keeping a log helps to make touring more interesting. Rough notes can be made on tour and copied into a loose-leaf logbook at home. Photographs or sketches can be associated with the notes in the logbook.

Once the touring area is chosen the explorer can consider other matters. A train or steamer journey may be necessary to reach the beginning of the tour. Time-tables and fares must be studied. Although travel expenses are high, they may be a necessary evil. Taking a cycle by train or boat is quite simple, and often adds memorable experiences to the tour. Where shops are likely to be scarce make sure that there is plenty of room for extra food.

Make a list of the kit required, and gather the items together a week or two in advance. Have a full dress-rehearsal to find the best way of packing everything. *Remember the general arrangement, and pack things in the same order each day.* A change of clothing can be posted in advance, addressed to oneself at the *Poste Restante* of a town through which the explorer will pass. Soiled clothing can be sent home from the same Post Office. Do not forget to fit a cyclometer if the mileage is to be checked. Although miles are of secondary importance, it is always interesting to know the distance covered. Examine lighting equipment, and consider gears and tyres. If cycle exploring abroad is the plan then roadster tyres of the same size will help to soften the bumpy *pavé* in many continental towns, while in the mountains of Switzerland a bottom gear of about 30 in. will be needed.

Every Youth Club, Youth Hostel local branch, Scout Group and Girl Guide company can have its own Cycling Section. Cycle exploring does not need a team to make the game interesting. It may be desirable to divide the section into two, one for the stronger riders and another for the potterers. A set of rules can be drawn up but the leader must always ensure that the rules are observed strictly. No member ought to be permitted to break away from the cycling section while on a run. Appoint an experienced cyclist as leader and elect a small committee for the purpose of arranging details. The leader need not lead the runs, but his duties can include the checking of members' machines to ensure that they are roadworthy, *and* calling members to order when they break the rules!

Once the Cycling Section has been launched all kinds of runs can be arranged, including week-end Youth Hostel outings. Keeping a Section log is an ideal way of recording cycling activities. It may look neatest if the notes are typewritten or written in the same handwriting; but the leader of each day's journey can prepare the report for inclusion in the log.

The pleasures of cycle exploring cannot be expressed in words: but anyone, young or old, with a spirit of adventure, sufficient knowledge to maintain a bicycle in good running order, intelligent enough to want to know more about the country-side, and happy when in the open air will really enjoy every minute of every cycle run.

Remember, cycle exploring is especially productive of results when carried out with young people. Their enthusiasm, verve and eagerness "to learn and know" are well suited to the rhythm and variety of cycle touring. In this chapter I have taken a personal view of cycle exploring but the technique is readily adaptable to party touring.

FURTHER READING

Cycling Manual, 1968—R. John Way (Temple Press)
Cycling for You—Ronald English (Lutterworth Press)

Teach Yourself Cycling—R. C. Shaw (English Universities Press)
The Complete Cyclist—Harold Moore (Pitman)
Cycles and Cycling—H. J. Way (Brown, Son & Ferguson)
Know the Game—Cycling (Educational Productions Ltd.)

An out-of-print title which is still very useful and may be found in second-hand bookshops is:
Adventure Cycling—Ronald English (Nicholas Kaye)

CHAPTER 5

Exploring by Water

IF we look at almost any One-inch O.S. map of Britain we find
blue lines indicating waterways all over it, showing that none
of us are far from water of some sort. Yet how much do we
know of our waterways? Even in the most thickly populated
towns there are canals, about which most of the population are
ignorant. If we are looking for an adventurous holiday, a voy-
age in a small boat can give us something to remember.

Of course, we are not allowed on every piece of water shown
on the map. Much of it is private, but there are many thousands
of miles open to us. We are free to go anywhere that the tide
flows—with a few exceptions, such as R.A.F. bombing ranges,
where we would not want to go in any case. That means that
we can go all round the coast, and up any inlet or river estuary
as far as the highest tide reaches, without asking permission.
For instance, on the Thames we are free to go up through
London as far as Teddington Lock ("Tide-end-town"). On
some rivers, such as those on the flat East coast, it is difficult to
tell exactly where the tide ends, but except for one or two
broads there is no difficulty about boating on the non-tidal
parts.

Non-tidal water is assumed to belong to the owners of the
banks—divided down the middle if there are two owners. In a
similar manner to many footpaths over private ground, a legal
right of way has been established on some rivers through long
usage—in many cases dating back to coracles. On very many
other rivers where there may not be a legal right of way, the
owners have never objected to boating. Some rivers where we

may boat on the non-tidal as well as the tidal parts, without restriction, are: the River Wye, from Hay; the River Avon, from Stratford; the River Severn, from Pool Quay; the River Ouse from Bedford.

Sometimes the river has only been made navigable by the building of weirs and locks, and the people who have done this work are entitled to payment. In most cases the fee is only very small—for instance, on the Severn the canoeist may arrive at a massive lock and for a few pence be passed through with enough water to float a sea-going vessel. In some cases a registration fee is necessary, and on the Thames this has now replaced lock fees. The Thames Conservancy whose address is 15 Buckingham Street, London, W.C.2, issues an annual registration for a canoe for £1 4s., but a triennial registration fee may be had for £3 which to an enthusiastic canoeist will represent better value for money. These fees will enable the canoeist to use all locks from Cricklade to Teddington free of toll charges.

The legal position on lakes is similar to that affecting rivers. Many are privately-owned and not available but on others boats and canoes may ply without permission. Some owners require a small fee. The position should be checked carefully in each case before using; if in doubt consult the local police personally or by telephone.

Besides the natural waterways there is a network of canals These were made mostly about a century ago. Some still prosper and carry heavy commercial traffic. Others have occasional use, while many are disused, but are still passable to the adventurous-minded in suitable craft. Permission *must* be obtained to use any canal. Licences are obtainable from the British Waterways Board, Willow Grange, Church Road, Watford, Hertfordshire, for periods of one week, one month, or three, six, nine or twelve months.

*   *   *

At most river locks the work is done by a lock-keeper, but on canals the locks are worked by the canoeist. For this a

E

A canal lock showing a detail of the key for opening the gates

crank handle, usually called a "windlass", is used to operate the sluices for "paddles". Generally it is possible to hire a windlass at the start of the canal. This fits a square shaft, usually about 1 in. square, but sizes vary on some canals.

A lock provides a sort of water lift from one level to another; but on a first visit its working may appear a little mysterious. The ends of the lock are closed by gates, either single or double, pointing towards the higher level, so that the pressure of the water keeps them shut. Either on the gates or in the lock sides are posts carrying racks and pinions. The windlass fits the shaft of the pinion. Suppose we arrive at the bottom of a lock and find it open—we take our boat in and shut the bottom gates, then lower all the paddles at the lower end. At the top end we open the paddles slowly. If we let the water in with a rush a small boat might be swamped. When the water inside the lock is the same as that above the top gates, then we open them and pass through. Coming down we do the same thing in reverse, and if we find the lock full when we want it empty, or vice versa, we must prepare it first. Lock gates will not move until the water level is exactly the same at both sides.

Rivers which have not been made navigable by the building of locks flow naturally and nearly always have rapids and falls in their courses. These provide the greatest fun to the explorer in a canoe or other small craft. Usually the water bubbles and froths and can be heard rushing over the stones before we come to it. If it is straight and simple we head for the V of smooth water which nearly always points the way into the deepest channel, and keeps going with the current. If we think we may ground in a shallow rapid we approach it "backwatering", and if we do touch we step out smartly and get to the stern, then let the canoe float in front of us to deeper water. If there are any snags, we land and inspect the rapid, and if it is doubtful we line down the boat at one side—letting the boat float through while we hold the stern painter and wade after it. This routine is recommended and followed by an expert canoeist in P.W. Blandford.

Coastal cruising is for the more ambitious and experienced. While the beginner may tackle some of the inland waters in the craft of his choice and hope to learn as he goes, he needs to be master of his craft and possess a fair knowledge of seamanship before attempting a cruise in open waters in a small boat. The best way to learn salt water cruising is to spend a holiday boating in a large harbour or land-locked estuary, such as Poole or Chichester harbours or the estuary of the Dart. A sailing dinghy is one of the best craft for this sort of cruising, while decked canoes make surprising passages in capable hands.

We can explore by water almost anything that floats, providing we realize its possibilities and limitations, and pick a trip which suits the craft. Here are notes on some of the commoner small boats:

Punts. These can be hired from many places on the Thames and similar placid rivers. A punt is roomy and can be fitted with a camping cover so that up to four can sleep on board in reasonable comfort. A punt cannot be portaged easily and is only suitable for calm waters. It is rather slow, and a cruise with a punt should be planned as a rather leisurely enterprise. Where the depth of the water and the state of the bottom permit, a punt can be poled, but this is not simple for young people to learn. Canoe paddles can be used, and where there is a towpath, a long tow-rope provides a change of exercise.

Skiffs. These may also be hired from the same places as punts, and are suitable for similar water conditions. Being propelled by oars or sculls, they are much faster and capable of longer dis-

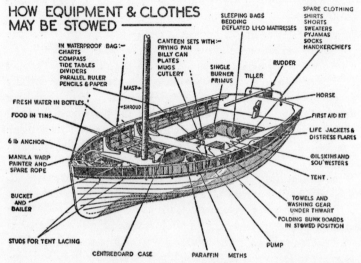

Dinghy camping demands "a place for everything, and everything in its place", or chaos abounds. Here is a well-tried plan for stowing equipment and clothes in a dinghy

tances. It is possible to fit camping covers to skiffs, but because of their shape it is impossible to sleep as many on board as can be carried during the day. The difficulty can be overcome by carrying shore camping kit for some of the party.

Dinghies. These are shorter and tubbier than skiffs. The shape is more seaworthy and rough water can be tackled. River dinghies sometimes have removable thwarts, so that two can sleep in comfort under a camping cover. For cruising in open water a sailing dinghy provides plenty of sport, and a tent rigged over the boom will provide protection for the night in a sheltered anchorage.

Canoes. These are the most popular craft for exploring by

water. A canoe is light in weight and of such a shallow draught that it will almost float on a bit of damp ground! It can be used in waters inaccessible to other craft, and when an obstruction is reached, portaging is usually easy. The traditional open Canadian canoe may be hired on a number of waterways. The single-bladed paddling technique is soon learnt. The "Canadian" is a good load-carrier and can give young people a holiday with all the romantic atmosphere of the old-time pioneers.

Decked kayak-type canoes are now more popular than the Canadian canoe. They can be folding or rigid, professionally or home made. The skin is usually of canvas, and a seaworthy craft can be built for a few pounds by anyone with a few tools and a little skill. The decked canoe may be a single- or a two-seater, and is propelled by double-bladed paddles, which are easier to use than single-bladed. There is ample room below the decks for camping kit. Excellent plans for making a number of single- and two-seater canoes, specially designed by P. W. Blandford, are available and may be obtained from Quinton House, Newbold-on-Stour, Stratford-on-Avon, Warwickshire.

Other craft. All the craft so far described are fairly small, and depend on the efforts of the crew for progress. Nearly all of them may be fitted with an outboard motor, which has its uses in some circumstances, but there is much more satisfaction in getting somewhere by your own efforts. For larger craft there is more of a case for power. On some waterways a motor cruiser can provide a base for a fleet of smaller craft, and be the means of towing them from place to place.

A sailing yacht, with a cabin, has the advantage of providing shelter, and for open water of a good depth a sailing yacht has some possibilities. For a yacht to sail well it must have a good depth of keel, either fixed or as a hinged centre board, so there are limits to this sort of boating.

*　　　*　　　*

The traditional craft on our canals are "narrow boats", often mistakenly called "barges". These may be horse-drawn, but it is more common now for boats to travel in pairs, with one power boat towing its unpowered "butty". Some narrow boats have been converted to passenger carrying, and are available for fairly large parties to explore the canals.

It is possible to cruise on some waters and find overnight accommodation ashore, but this ties the party to fixed stops. If we can sleep aboard our craft or carry camping kit we become independent, and most small-boat explorers find this the most attractive method. With most craft we can carry more camping kit than we should if we were hiking or cycling. The only time we need consider paring our kit to a minimum is when a trip involves many portages.

Normal fairly lightweight camping equipment is needed. Waterproof kit-bags are more useful than rucksacks, and it is an advantage to divide the kit up into small bags for stowage. If we are sleeping on board, air beds or some other means of padding the floor are essential. During the day, a partly inflated air bed in a waterproof bag will give our craft extra buoyancy in case of emergency.

If we hope to travel far it is best to take our largest meals at breakfast and supper, with just a light snack at mid-day. With almost every meal at a different place a pressure stove is much more convenient than a fire for cooking, although an occasional wood-fire is very pleasant in the evenings. A pressure cooker makes the cook's job relatively easy for a youth group. Its use is now accepted in all forms of camping.

Clothing is most important on a boating holiday. *Take plenty of it!* Apart from any risk of a ducking, temperatures on the water vary between swimming-trunk conditions and near-Arctic, or at least Icelandic, temperatures. A lightweight oilskin coat and a sou'wester are best for wet weather. For protection against cold winds one of the proofed anoraks or Grenfell jackets is needed.

When planning a cruise consider the accessibility of the water if your craft has to be transported. Most small boats can be sent fairly cheaply by rail. If your boat will go in the train's luggage van you can even take it as ordinary luggage! Alternatively, it may travel on the roof of a car, or behind it on a trailer.

Most beginners tend to be too ambitious in their projects.

On calm water a skiff may be rowed twenty-five miles in a day. Fifteen miles is more reasonable for a canoe, and a punt only about half that. If you pass a large number of locks, they will shorten the distance considerably. If portaging locks as well, a dozen will be plenty to pass in a day. Most of us go exploring by water to get away from the bustle of the roads. We must keep distances short, and allow plenty of time for seeing the country-side through which we are passing.

Keep a log at all times. Let this be a note-book containing times and distances, but also put down anything of interest which you see. Add sketches and maps, and stick in photographs and picture post cards. The result, no matter how simple, will jog the memory in delightful fashion in future years.

*　　*　　*

Information on waterways must be obtained in advance from various sources. There is no one book which explains everything. The biggest book is *Inland Waterways of Great Britain and Northern Ireland* by L. A. Edwards, published by Imray, Laurie, Norie and Wilson. This contains details and itineraries of all the rivers and canals suitable for larger craft. It does not deal with the smaller waters only accessible to craft which can be portaged. Stanford's *Inland Cruising Map of England* is drawn to a scale of eight miles to one inch. This also only shows waters suitable for larger craft, but it shows the position of all locks—an important consideration, particularly on canals. Stanford's also publish a strip map of the River Thames to a scale of $1\frac{1}{2}$ inches to one mile.

The most comprehensive guide to all waters suitable for small boats is the *Guide to the Waterways of the British Isles*, published by the British Canoe Union. This can only be bought by members of clubs affiliated to the B.C.U. For non-members the best information on rivers suitable for canoeing will be found in *Canoeing* by W. Bliss, published by Methuen. Some clubs, magazines and canoe manufacturers issue itineraries of the more popular rivers.

Anyone wishing to cruise on salt water should get the appropriate charts. There are special charts issued for yachtsmen and obtainable through yacht chandlers and nautical booksellers. The One-inch O.S. maps provide a good guide to the country-side generally, and any cruise is made more interesting by studying these maps as well as any specialized information on the waters. Waterproof map cases are essential at times, and can be made at home or school, in the leathercraft class, with "Perspex" fronts.

Canoeing Kit. As a guide to anyone planning a boating holiday, the following is a list of the kit carried by P. W. Blandford on canoe-camping cruises for two people.

1. Two single-seat canoes, fitted with spray covers which closed the cockpit completely at night. Box seats. Compass on bracket at side of cockpit. Repair kit. Football bladders pushed in each end for reserve buoyancy.
2. Six small kit-bags made of rubberized material. These are sealed by tying around the neck, then doubling over and tying again.
3. Clothing. Shirt, shorts and underclothes as normal wear; duplicate sets for emergency. Shoes and stockings. Old plimsolls for wading. Sweaters. Anoraks. Sou'westers and short oilskin jackets to fit outside the spray covers. Plastic raincoats for use ashore. Sun glasses. Small first-aid kit. Clothes-mending material. Handkerchiefs. Swimming trunks.
4. Normal washing gear. Canvas bowl. Extra towel packed with spare clothes for emergency use. Toilet paper. Trowel.
5. Two sleeping bags. Pyjamas. Air beds. Torch or Hand-lamp with spare batteries. Candles for emergency.
6. Lightweight ridge tent with fitted groundsheet for preference.
7. Two folding pressure stoves. One canteen consisting of two pots and a frying-pan. Matches in waterproof container. One quart can paraffin. Two quart water bottles. Small canvas bucket. Cutlery, including a small bread saw and a key-style tin opener. Unbreakable mugs and plates. Drying cloth or tea towel.
8. Note-book, pencil, ball pen, stamped post cards, maps,

itineraries. Money (best carried in a pouch on the belt with more in waterproof bag). Camera.

9. Food, mostly in metal and plastic containers. Bread and perishable food in linen, plastic or "Porosan" bags.

*   *   *

The river Thames is in many ways ideal for an actual boating holiday, but this is only one good idea. Think of the many fine rivers in all parts of Britain which are suitable for this kind of camping. Let us not neglect our waterways when planning exploring trips or holidays for they offer abundant adventure and a wealth of interesting activities.

FURTHER READING

Holidays Afloat—Percy W. Blandford (Lutterworth Press)

Canoes and Canoeing—Percy W. Blandford (Lutterworth Press)

Small Boats and Sailing—Percy W. Blandford (Lutterworth Press)

Canoeing—W. Bliss (Methuen)

Inland Waterways of Great Britain and Northern Ireland—L. A. Edwards (Imray, Laurie, Norie and Wilson)

Guide to the Waterways of the British Isles (British Canoe Union)

The Seaside Nature Book—Eric Fitch Daglish (Dent)

SECTION B

WHAT TO DO—OUTDOOR PROJECTS

CHAPTER 6

Animal Watching

WHERE the stream broadened out to meet the tide, a grove of willows huddled round the briar-tangled ruins of a lime-kiln which stood at the brow of the precipitous bank. The pale tense light of the spring evening was still filtering through the trees when, at the fringe of the pool, there appeared a round, fierce-whiskered face which, but for the bright eyes gleaming in it, might have been a piece of jetsam, so smoothly did it come drifting. Behind it, two smaller shapes followed, imitating every movement of the first.

It was a bitch otter and her two cubs.

Suddenly the otter dived; she was barely gone a moment or two when up she came again, a small fish visible in her mouth. Eagerly pursued by the cubs, she made her way to shallower water where, with a toss of her round, bewhiskered head, she dropped her catch. A wild scramble ensued. One of the cubs secured it and took it to the bank and hunched over it, driving off his brother—or sister, whichever was the case—with a grown-up snarl that must almost have dislocated his puny jaws.

But the cubs had apparently been well fed already, for presently they scampered a little way up the bank, while the bitch otter rolled in the kingcups at the edge of the stream and then sat up to scratch.

The cubs evidently knew this muddy bank well: with paws splayed out and miniature rudders trailing, they slid merrily down one after the other into the water.

Whistling in appreciation of this game, they swam round and clambered out; shook themselves, scampered up the bank again and once more slithered down the slide. The fun waxed fast and furious. One of the cubs followed too closely on the tail of his brother. The pair of them tumbled over and over in a furry tangle and bumped into their mother, who cuffed them amiably and rolled them in the mud. . .

All that is not the beginning of a story. It was rewritten from a Nature note-book kept by a skilled and patient animal watcher, Alan C. Jenkins. He was lying hidden among the ivy and brambles that shrouded the crumbling lime-kiln wall. For more than a fortnight he had spent part of almost every night on a Devon stream looking for those otters. He had come across various signs of them along the stream: their "seals" or prints at the edge of the water; the tell-tale streak in the sand where the bitch otter had dragged her long rudder; remains of the roach she had caught. But not until that evening did he actually see anything of them; nor did he see them again. Nevertheless, the indescribable thrill of those few brief moments amply rewarded him, for they were among the most enjoyable "animal watchings" he had experienced. Alan Jenkins had seen what comparatively few other people have witnessed—one of the shyest of wild animals hunting and playing. However briefly, he had, for a short while, entered another world.

*   *   *

At first sight there may not seem a lot of scope for animal watching in Britain, but though the lives of animals in Britain are, perhaps, not as spectacular as those of the creatures of Arctic tundra or tropical jungle, there is just as much drama in the raiding party of weasels spreading terror among the voles and shrews of the hedgerows as the wolf-pack harrying the reindeer of Lapland; just as much drama in the hedgehog tackling the viper as there is in the nimble mongoose battling with the deadly hamadryad. It is, surely, only a matter of degree. The mild British country-side is, in its own small way, another jungle, and the lives of its denizens are full of thrilling episodes.

No one can hope to see all the details of this never-endin

drama of river and hill and copse, but anyone prepared to make the effort may catch glimpses of it. The trouble they take will be richly compensated, for animal watching is one of the most exciting and rewarding of pastimes, being, like so many other worthwhile things, a mixture of skill and patience, together with a dash of good luck. Naturally there are easier opportunities for the country-dweller, yet for the townsman there are summer evenings, week-ends, and holidays.

Even in and near London and other big towns there are certain opportunities: foxes have been recorded in Kenwood and Hampstead Heath, for example (and since World War II they have developed a keen interest in the dustbins of North-West London). In Richmond Park a great deal of pleasure can be had studying deer, though we give them a healthy berth during the autumn rut, for the stags can be awkward customers when they are in a bad temper. Simply sitting under a haystack or by a canal can produce results: the mole emerging from his tunnel for a breath of fresh air—or to chase some rival, which he sometimes does to the point of starvation; the demure water-vole—usually slandered by being miscalled "water-rat"—quietly enjoying a succulent stem of loosestrife. Or if we are camping, while we are settling down for the night it is both instructive and amusing to try and identify the different sounds: the soft, wheezing conversational grunt of the hedgehog; the eerie scream of the vixen; the irascible hissing-squeak of the shrew; the alarm-bark of the deer; the clear whistle of the otter.

One great advantage of animal watching is that it can be done with a minimum of material equipment. Old clothes are the most obvious necessity for roughing it in hills and woods, though do not imagine that animal watching is a matter of crawling about commando-fashion: if we do that we shall only succeed in making a noise like a herd of cattle, scaring every living thing within hearing. Incidentally, while mentioning "don'ts", *don't trespass*! Most reasonable people will give us permission to enter their land if we ask them; but they rightly tend to resent unauthorized intrusion.

Binoculars are useful for long-range work—watching deer on the hills or seals on the shore, for example—but for close-range observation they are unnecessary and at times even a hindrance, for often the very act of fiddling about with them will be enough to startle the animal we are watching.

A humble item of equipment which will increase the pleasure and value of animal watching tenfold is simply a note-book. Animal watching without keeping a record of our observations is rather like playing cricket without bothering to keep the score. The human memory is very fallible and we can write up our notes as soon as possible after the actual watching time. Skilled animal watchers can write up their first impressions roughly and then transcribe them to something more permanent later. Gradually they build up a fascinating personal journal of nature through the seasons, and such note-books become among our most cherished possessions.

We can keep records of individual themes in which we become interested: we can make a study of hibernation—deciding on our own evidence whether or not the badger hibernates; or where the hedgehog spends the winter; or we can discover the little hoards of nuts and berries that squirrel and dormouse lay up. From our observations on the food that various animals eat we can develop an interesting study of their economic relation to agriculture: does the good the stoat performs in killing pests such as rabbits and rats outweigh the occasional egg-stealing and chick-killing he may do? Is the mole beneficial or otherwise? Is the badger ever guilty of killing lambs or does he get the blame for crimes perpetrated by the fox? All these and other bits of detective work will make our record keeping a fascinating hobby.

But, enjoyable though the note-book is, the most essential equipment in animal watching is of a mental kind: we need to be equipped with unbounded patience. If we have not got that or are not prepared to cultivate it, then we can straightaway give up the idea of adopting animal watching as a hobby. We have to be prepared for a lot of discomfort, for many blank days and nights, and then, perhaps, when the object of our watching has at last appeared, for all our patient effort to be ruined by some chance passer-by or garrulous magpie. Animals take nothing on trust; every moment they are risking their lives and

Part of the research programme at Slapton Lea in Devonshire, where monthly samples of the fish population are taken with seine nets (Diana Peile).

Pools left dry by the tide teem with marine life, and give ample scope for close study at Watchet, Somerset. (Below) a field study group checking and identifying pond specimens (both G. R. Swift).

to say that they are ultra-cautious is an understatement. If, however, we intend to become skilled, we shall be determined to win what is to a great extent a battle of wits—for it is a contest between our skill in woodcraft and the animal's instinct of self-preservation.

The first practical knowledge to acquire is where to seek the creatures in which we are interested: as in most things, it is better to start in a modest way to avoid being discouraged. Any old belfry or barn will provide us with ample material in the way of bats, for instance: and we shall soon discover that they are not merely "bats", for there are twelve distinct kinds in Britain, ranging from the Noctule or Great Bat, which has a wing-span of fourteen inches, to the tiny Pipistrelle or Common Bat, whose head and body measure little more than one and a half inches. Record the times of their emerging in conjunction with the temperature and the season of the year. The neighbourhood of a farmyard will give us plenty of scope. We can set ourselves the task of identifying the various kinds of mice and voles. We shall be surprised to find how many species there are: bank-vole, field-vole, water-vole, wood-mouse, harvest-mouse, dormouse, and so on.

Books and zoos and museums can teach us a certain amount about where to look and how to identify, but it is on our own slow, painstaking experience that we must rely most, though there are other sources of information which are both profitable and enjoyable: the shepherd keeping his lonely watch on the downs; the forester in the plantation; the riverkeeper going his rounds; the tractor-driver mowing the last swaths; all such people will prove a rich source of local wild-lore if we get to know them. Even the local poacher can be useful at times; indeed, very useful!

It was a shepherd who taught Alan Jenkins that a hare can see anything to the side and to the rear, but nothing directly ahead, which is why we may find a hare running swiftly and straight towards us. A gamekeeper taught him how to whistle-up his own animal watching (though he did it for a different purpose): he would put a blade of grass between his hands and,

F

blowing on it, imitate the squeal of a rabbit. This would have an irresistible effect on any stoat or fox that happened to be in the neighbourhood.

Parallel with learning where to *look*, we must learn to *observe*, to correlate the experience of all the senses, of sight, of hearing, of smell. Train ourselves to ask the reason for the different clues we come across: why *was* that hare cantering *down*wind? It would only do that if it was frightened. Normally an animal runs *into* the wind to catch any message of danger the latter may bear. Stand still and we may see what is pursuing the hare. Those vertical claw-marks on the sycamore: could they have been made by a badger reaching up to stretch before setting out on his nocturnal round? Or if it is a young tree, possibly it is a hare or a deer that has been "barking" it? Those shreds of pine-cones scattered about: have squirrels been at work? There may be a "drey" or nest in one of the nearby trees.

Why is the grass slowly springing up again? Something has trodden it down obviously. Why is that magpie having so much to say? It can't be the keeper; we passed him in the village just now: perhaps there's a fox doing a daytime prowl, which is really quite a common occurrence. The fox makes a first-class animal-watching study.

*   *   *

The most enjoyable—and also the most arduous—animal watching is to keep regular watch on the home of one particular animal. The badger is an excellent example, for it prefers to occupy the same premises more or less permanently (and some badger diggings have existed for centuries), whereas fox and otter tend to change their quarters frequently, particularly the latter, because it is a great wanderer. The fox, being of a lazy disposition, will often take up lodgings in a badger's sett, as it is called, until its filthy habits rouse the righteous indignation of the landlord!

Once we have found a sett, either by local information or by the cart-loads of soil the occupants have dug out, or by the well-defined paths that lead from it, we shall have to turn up at least an hour before the badger usually emerges, which is twilight or even later (though there is nothing it likes better than basking in the sun on its special sunning-platform). Generally speaking, animals are very regular in their habits, but circumstances arise which alter their routine. The badger detests wet weather, and if the previous evening has been rainy it may have stayed at home, in which case it will venture out all the earlier the following night.

Always make an approach from the leeward, even if it means making a long detour; otherwise the badger, who, like most wild animals, depends far more on its sense of smell than on its eyesight, which isn't particularly good, will stay put. Its patience is far greater than ours can ever be, for its life depends on it. Brock takes no chances if he's in doubt!

The first thing to do when we reach the neighbourhood of the sett is to make ourselves comfortable. If we are going to do the job properly we may have to spend several hours in the same position, and that is the hardest part of animal watching. Occasionally there will be a convenient tree into which you can climb, or a ferny bank on which to sit, but if it is at all possible, a skilled animal watcher likes to stand upright: not of course so that his body is silhouetted, but preferably in front of a tree. Not only does one merge with the tree, which the badger is used to seeing, but also an upright position is by far the most comfortable, for it is possible to lean against the tree and shift the weight from one foot to the other without any perceptible movement.

But however comfortable the animal watcher makes himself, there is one foe in animal watching that he cannot avoid, at least in summer: insects, and especially midges! Those tiny, almost invisible, creatures are the bane of the animal watcher. They are a hair-raising—and bump-raising—torment, and it is no use applying one or other of many preparations: we might as well shout down one of the tunnels and announce our arrival to the nearest badger. Incidentally, we have to bear in mind that those tunnels, being larger at the mouth than inside, act in the same way as an ear-trumpet, so that the slightest sound is amplified to the badger wondering whether it is safe to emerge!

However, if we are prepared to endure cramp and midges,

blank nights and various other frustrations, we shall not go un-rewarded, for something is always happening in nature, even if the object of our vigil decides to sulk. Alan Jenkins went once to watch badgers and witnessed instead a squirrel making a smash-and-grab raid on a jay's nest (both notorious predators!) and being caught red-handed by the irate birds, who raised such a hullabaloo that within a matter of moments practically every bird in the wood must have been mobbing that unfortunate squirrel.

We may watch the same badger sett night after night with-out result . . . and then at last known the thrill and triumph of seeing a black-and-white striped head wavering cautiously up from the tunnel and then . . . the emergence of a sow-badger followed by plump, jostling cubs who almost blunder over our feet in their play. The same sow-badger may be seen bust-ling about her spring-cleaning, dragging out great bundles of badger "hay" and fetching fresh bracken. The badger is the most fastidious of animals and keeps its home scrupulously clean.

More details of my own animal-watching in relation to foxes and badgers in the 1963–8 period are published in my recent book *Lightweight Camping* (Lutterworth Press).

＊   ＊   ＊

Certainly night is the most exciting time (though of course the most difficult), but there is plenty of scope for animal watch-ing in day-time, especially in the evening and early morning. Foxes may be seen giving their cubs a hunting lesson soon after tea-time, and have come so close to an animal watcher that he could have touched them. In broad daylight a stoat has been seen rolling over and over in the most incredible antics, trying to lure a group of birds off their guard so that he could get within reach.

On the moors and hills the red deer are often active in day-light, while on the coast of Scotland or East Anglia there is the chance of watching both grey and common seals harrying shoals of fish, and a thrilling sight this is, except perhaps to the local fishermen, for a pair of grey seals will work a shoal exactly like a pair of gun-dogs working a covey of partridge.

Nor is it only a matter of watching the larger animals. There is a lot of amusement to be had watching the antics of harvest mice squabbling for possession of a cornstalk—though unfortunately that delightful little creature is becoming rare; or the tiny water-shrew taking a header from his favourite diving-board and swimming furiously after whirligig beetles.

We shall not always see what we expect to see, nor find it where we should expect to find it: I have seen grey squirrels living in rabbit burrows, and heard of foxes playing with rabbits in quite ridiculous fashion. Some animals will reveal themselves through sheer curiosity: weasel and stoat especially are incurably, and sometimes fatally, inquisitive, and often when they should be scurrying to safety they cannot resist returning for a second look, peering out at one intently from woodstack or bank.

Snow is a profitable time for the animal watcher, when hunger makes wild creatures less cautious, and their comings and goings on their lawful or unlawful occasions can be read like a page in a book. An animal watcher who lived in the Highlands remembers the excitement of gradually getting to know the different tracks that surrounded his "but-and-ben"—otherwise cottage —in very cold weather, unravelling the intricate pattern, making sketches and keeping a "dossier" of every animal, until eventually he could tell whether that track across the frozen loch was made by a fox running fast . . . an otter enjoying a slide through the snow . . . a hare leaping in order to break his trail and deceive the pursuing ermine . . . or a roebuck in search of his neighbour's meagre haystack.

But winter or summer, we shall find animal watching a never-ending delight, and a pastime which, once we have experienced it, we shall consider worth all the effort it entails. It is a clean and exciting sport, for we are pitting our wits and our woodcraft against the natural caution and cunning of wild creatures. Moreover, we are not destroying life, but watching it instead, and enriching our own experience of all the wonders of nature.

What is more, we are doing something for ourselves, which is incomparably better than sitting back and depending on someone else to provide artificial entertainment for us. This is an intensely important point to consider in all voluntary youth work with boys and girls.

*   *   *

Finally, I want to say something about my own squirrel watching, because there are probably more opportunities of watching the squirrel in Britain than any other wild animal, at least so far as young people are concerned.

My study of the squirrel and its habits, habitat and customs started in earnest when the late Captain C. H. Michaelson, R.N., verderer of Great Tower Plantation, near Windermere, showed me how to attract red squirrels to the window of his hut in the trees, about 6 a.m. on a very cold March morning. Captain Michaelson was a naturalist of rare distinction, especially skilled in the study of insects, but he had a way with most wild animals and birds, and in addition could teach young people a great deal about them in a short space of time.

His technique with the red squirrels at Great Tower was to open a hut window quietly in the early morning and gently tap on the ledge with shelled peanuts. Almost at once three red squirrels, one large male and two smaller females, would come across the clearing and climb the side of the hut to take the nuts from his fingers and then eat them on their haunches a few yards away. The routine continued each morning, and even when the females were heavy with young; I soon had no difficulty at all in persuading those attractive red squirrels to take shelled nuts from my own fingers, in the same way as Captain Michaelson.

Soon afterwards I became interested in the problem of the grey squirrel, the alien tree rat introduced so mistakenly into Britain in late Victorian times from North America. The grey squirrel spread rapidly because, apart from man himself, who did little about it, the animal had no natural enemies. (Its enemy, the pine marten, or tree weasel, was almost extinct.) There can be no doubt that the larger grey alien squirrel has driven out the smaller red native English squirrel, and in fact killed it whenever it had the chance. Moreover, there is ample evidence that the grey squirrel is undoubtedly a menace in forestry plantations, orchards, market gardens and private gardens, stripping young bark and damaging and eating tender young green foliage and shoots.

To my mind this was an excellent subject for study on treks by youth groups using lightweight camping equipment or youth hostels as a base. We would try and find out as much as we could about the grey squirrel menace. Even now, after twenty years, there are many problems unsolved as far as grey squirrels are concerned and our field note-books are far from complete. But we have done considerable original research and found out many things about grey squirrels we did not know before.

The first thing was to find an area where both grey and red squirrels were fairly common. We went to Central Wales and in the area around Oswestry–Bala–Llangollen found the right terrain. Wynnstay Park, Ruabon, was one of the original places where grey squirrels were released some seventy years ago. It was literally swarming with grey squirrels throughout World War II. But in the Tanat Valley, a delightful and little-known region some miles to the south, we found greys and reds living apparently in harmony. One summer afternoon I was trekking with young people along the banks of the Dee near Llangollen when I noticed a curious animal head in the river bank. Soon it was apparent there were a number of small animals swimming in the river. Careful watch was kept on them and before long they were seen to leave the water and climb the bank. Any suspicion that they might be rats was dispelled as soon as they climbed the nearest tree trunk. Without any shadow of doubt they were five grey squirrels.

Subsequent squirrel treks showed that grey squirrels were frequently seen swimming in the Dee but always near the bank. In recent years I have often seen grey squirrels fording streams in Hertfordshire, and on two occasions swimming downstream with the current. In the Tanat Valley in 1942 we recorded red squirrels splashing in a stream, and swimming in shallow water about nine inches deep. That was the first occasion, but by 1970 the number of sightings was impressive.

So we had at least proved that squirrels could swim, a fact
that had previously been doubted in some quarters, but it
needed much continuous observation on trek to get the facts.
Swimming seems more prevalent in dry summers.

Grey squirrels raid birds' nests, taking eggs and young.
There is no doubt about it at all. They have been photographed
in the act. The red squirrel, of course, is not a blameless creature
and will damage conifers in much the same way as the grey, but
his depredations are negligible by comparison. We found some
very strange facts about the diet of grey squirrels.

They will readily desert a diet of acorns, nuts and tree shoots
for a crumbly, warm mash made for poultry and containing
meat or fish meal, and this at all times of the year. The grey
squirrel is *not* a true hibernator, and though it may sleep for
fairly lengthy periods it can be found as active as ever all
through the winter months, particularly in wet "green" winters.
In 1952 we recorded them out and about on every day of the
year in south Hertfordshire, and again in 1957, 1959, 1961,
1965 and 1966. In the severe winter of 1962-3 there was not a
sign of squirrels but early in the cold spell they were seen many
times clambering over roof-tops and entering house lofts for
long periods through holes made by nesting starlings in the
previous spring. This continued every winter afterwards. On
one November day I recorded a tiny young grey in my own
garden only three inches long.

The boldness of greys and their increasing tendency towards
"domesticity" can be seen in the way they scale drain-pipes and
build nests in the roofs of suburban houses, particularly in
north-west London. The research of young people into this
habit showed that in the case of one detached house one or more
greys would scale a drain-pipe and systematically search under
eaves at all times of the year for the nests of sparrows and other
small birds. The most common time for this activity was early
morning and at roosting time. The fact that it was carried on
all the year round shows the determination of the grey. On
cold winter mornings and late afternoons, with a hard frost
underfoot, I have recorded grey squirrels huddling against
chimney stacks for warmth on the roofs of houses in Hertford-

shire. By all the laws of Nature the grey squirrels should have been hibernating in a tree-top drey fast asleep!

There are other curious anomalies in diet as far as the grey squirrel is concerned. It can strip a cherry tree in no time (as I know to my cost each year) but birds are just as big culprits. I have already instanced the way in which greys would eat a mash of meat or fish meal in preference to anything else. Young greys also have a great liking for toast! They will carry the toast if cut into "fingers" high into a drey even, and come down time and again for more.

In 1952 we actually recorded three grey squirrels eating the carcass of a chicken in broad moonlight in a spinney in Hertfordshire. For some time we had suspected that grey squirrels, fond as they are of young birds in spring and summer, will eat carrion, especially in winter. On this occasion the carcass of the chicken was left on the floor of the spinney deliberately on bright moonlit nights. Squirrels were seen to descend trees and tackle the bird in earnest, and, when disturbed by a powerful torch, disappear up the trunk of a Scots pine. The month was January and there was a hard, keen frost underfoot.

In several subsequent years squirrels were noted eating carrion, particularly birds and hedgehogs killed on country roads. In 1965 two squirrels were surprised feeding off a dead cat on a January afternoon.

Spring fights between large male greys occur frequently and are always worth watching. The enormous leaps and bounds are almost unbelievable unless one has seen such a fight. Occasionally one grey will fall to earth like a stone. A wounded grey is not a pleasant customer and a Press report from Kent in 1951 stated that a small child had been attacked and bitten by a wounded grey squirrel. It is quite easy to trap them in the long American-style rat traps placed at the foot of trees in which dreys are seen. The most suitable bait appears to be cheeserind. At least it does not fail to attract them!

The most modern method of shooting greys is to organize squirrel shooting parties in the late autumn or winter when all the leaves have fallen from the trees. The party borrows a telescopic metal pole, which has sections screwing into each other. The poles can usually be borrowed from the County Pest Office (not *Post* Office, please!). The dreys are then poked out and the squirrels shot as they appear on the surrounding branches. The odd thing about this method is that many dreys are apparently untenanted, lending support to the growing theory that greys are becoming more "domesticated" and seeking warm, dry winter quarters in barn roofs and even housetops. On the other hand as many as seven squirrels have been ejected from one drey, and shot.

The Ministry of Agriculture was so concerned about the grey squirrel problem that it offered "a bob a tail" for all grey squirrels killed in 1953. More than 250,000 greys were exterminated and £6,500 paid out in tail money.

At all events a long-term "Operation Grey Squirrel" has given a considerable number of youth groups and trekking parties some really good fun and useful field experience.

FURTHER READING

There are books of the calibre of *String Lug the Fox* by David Stephen and *Tarka the Otter* by Henry Williamson readily available, and a chat with the librarian of the local Public Library will invariably produce a long and detailed reading list. But, in my opinion, the most interesting reading is often to be found in the pages of the weekly journals, *Country Life* and *The Field*, and the quarterly journal, *The Countryman*, which is produced at Burford, Oxfordshire.

Recent books of especial interest include *Be a Nature Detective* by Maxwell Knight (Warne) and *Tracks* by E. A. R. Ennion and N. Tinbergen (Oxford University Press). One of the best modern handbooks on animal watching is *Wild Animals of the British Isles*, by Dr. Maurice Burton (Warne). This author's weekly notes in the *Daily Telegraph* on Saturdays are invaluable.

CHAPTER 7

Bird Watching

BIRD WATCHING is a first-class reason for running a lightweight camping or youth hostelling trek, or a canoeing trip, or a fell scramble. It gives the individual great personal rewards at no cost at all. The very fact that, like animal watching, it costs nothing is a prime reason for including it as an outdoor activity particularly suited to young people. It can be conducted all the year round and in every type of terrain. Some aspects of it, such as bird migration and feeding habits, will give a youth group enough work to do on trek for years on end.

Some young people have been frightened off bird watching by ornithological fanatics who may spend all their waking time in the pursuit of one rare or unusual bird, and thereby give the impression that years of intense study of technique and method are necessary before results can be obtained.

Young people can forget the rare birds, except when one crosses their path. The joy of good bird watching lies in the unexpected and the unknown. The ordinary everyday birds of moor, mountain, river and green field will give us all the fun in the world if we look for them.

At the outset it is wise to study the work and methods of bird watchers of repute, such as James Fisher, Bruce Campbell, Richard Fitter, Peter Scott, Charles Tunnicliffe, Maurice Burton and Eric Hosking. Standards of bird watching, can then be built up and a rough framework arranged for our own bird-watching camps and treks. Are we going to concentrate on birds of stream and river, or the hedgerows and open country, or cliff and rock face, or open sandy common, or rolling fell and moorland, or the gaunt, grey mountains themselves? Everything depends on the abilities, and experience, and inclinations, of the youth group concerned, and if the leader is in any doubt about it he or she can let the young people decide for themselves. Above all, they can be discouraged and disillusioned if they aim too high for a start. So we start quietly and "softlee", building up standards methodically and thoroughly until confidence, and knowledge, based on experience, are well-established.

If bird watching is to be fun the settings or terrain in which a bird was watched will remain as important as the bird itself. I first heard the long low "bubble" of a curlew in spring, surely the most beautiful of all mating calls, on a Lakeland fell on a perfect Easter Sunday. The setting was as important as the call. And there were ravens on South Stack at Holyhead, and mallard and widgeon winging across an estuary near Rhosneigr in the dusk of an August evening after rain—all quite unforgettable. I particularly love to watch finches in my own garden, noting what they feed on: goldfinches always on silver birch trunks in the early morning in summer and greenfinches deep in wisteria leaves, chaffinches drilling away in the lawn and the flash of bullfinches on seeding grasses and roses. Sparrows and blue tits go for my fruit tree buds, not the much-aligned bullfinch.

There is often real fun in bird watching, too, and the garrulous but canny magpie can be involved in that. I watched a magpie stalk a sitting rabbit feeding on my own lawn and gently tweak its tail. The rabbit leapt a full foot or more in the air ("like a startled hare" would be an apt cliché) turning completely around in its own tracks. For a moment the magpie and rabbit faced each other at a distance of a few feet before the rabbit made for the nearest hedge. Less than twenty minutes later the same magpie repeated the quick approach to another sitting rabbit, and again a tail was tweaked with gusto. This rabbit, angry and alarmed, chased the magpie until it gently took flight and disappeared into the spinney. It was spring-time. Did the magpie tweak for the sheer fun of it? Or did it fancy a rabbit's tail as a nest lining?

A distinguished bird watcher, Richard Fitter, says that the unexpected is always the best thing about a day's bird trek. He recalls a bright January day when he walked up the Exe estuary and saw a rare visitor to Britain in the spoonbill, and a fine evening in May when he came by chance upon a flock of 120 black tern on a reservoir in Hertfordshire. Truly they were red-letter days.

Boys and girls may well find their own ways of learning to spot the commoner birds on sight. Their eyes and ears are invariably good, and they are the first essentials in bird watching. I have seen a boy who was an expert plane-spotter bring his same skilled eye to bear on birds and identify them as quickly, especially when equipped with a good pair of Zeiss binoculars. Field glasses are not essential to good bird watching but they do make for keener observation and a greater interest in detail. Monoculars are also sold especially for bird watching but they need getting used to; a boy once told me they were "all right for one-eyed watchers".

There are a mass of good aids to bird watching. *Collins Pocket Guide to British Birds*, by R. S. R. Fitter (Revised Edition 1966) is so excellent that I recommend it whole-heartedly to any youth group. It has everything the young bird watcher needs—even more useful is *The Hamlyn Guide to British and European Birds* (Consultant Editor: Dr. Bruce Campbell, 1970). The location maps and illustrations by Arthur Singer are superb.

Imagine a camp site with half a dozen lightweight tents pitched in a half-moon on the edge of a Hampshire or Surrey wood on a week end in late spring. The dawn-chorus of the birds will waken many of the boys camping there. Bird watching becomes a sheer joy in such a sylvan setting. One does not even have to get out of bed! From the comfort of a down sleeping-bag the bird watcher needs only a pair of field-glasses and either of the two books recommended to spend a thoroughly enjoyable two hours before breakfast.

Canoeing brings its own rewards on many a navigable stream or canal or a small launch on the Norfolk Broads. But early morning bird watching from a tent is something for young people to learn and appreciate for themselves.

Richard Fitter's method works well with young people. He divides British birds into three broad groups: *Land*, *Waterside* and *Water*. Then within each group he arranges birds in order of size in eight grades based on the length of the bird from bill-tip to tail-tip. Each of these eight length-groups is typified by a common bird. If a boy or girl can judge the size of the bird seen then he or she has gone a long way towards its identification.

I asked Richard Fitter for advice suitable for young people on bird-watching treks:

"Once you have got a bird within good view", he told me, "it is important to know what features to look out for. Thus when you have an unknown wader flying past you, it is useful to know that wing-bars and rump-colour are keys to the identification of many of this group, whereas in the smaller birds of prey the shape of the wing and the colour of the mantle are what you should look out for. If you come and tell me that you have seen a small falcon with no wing-bar I cannot help you, for all three of the smaller British falcons you are likely to see have no wing-bar. If, however, you can tell me that it had a blue-grey head and tail and a chestnut mantle, I can say at once that it is a male kestrel, and not a hobby or merlin, nor even a sparrow-hawk. Until you know what features to look out for in each group, *it is best to observe all parts of the bird and make as full notes as possible.*"

That is sound and practical advice which will become more apparent as the observer grows in skill, wisdom and knowledge.

The question of note-making is important. It need not be emphasized too greatly at the beginning of the trek but by the third or fourth day the need for it will be obvious. It is best to let young people learn by practical experience. It may seem an absolute bore to them to have to keep field notes on bird watching at the beginning of an exciting lightweight camp trek. Before long they will find it a *necessity* because they are seeing and experiencing such a wealth of field study for themselves as they go on. They may wish to record it with camera or pencil and sketch-book, and even if they are novices at both mediums, they can practise until they make a fair shot at it.

POINTS TO BE NOTED

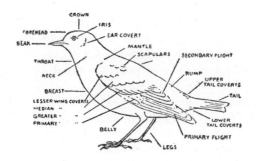

EXAMPLE OF USE OF THE DIAGRAMS

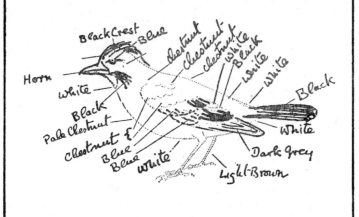

A specimen page of "The Bird-Watcher's Field Pocket-Book".
Other pages of the book give blank diagrams similar to the top one on
this page against which details may be written. It is an invaluable little
book for the amateur ornithologist and all youth groups on trek

What matters in all field work with young people is the amount of effort and enthusiasm put into it, and not necessarily the technical standard achieved. That will come in its own time.

*   *   *

The most satisfactory field note-book is simply a pocket-size loose-leaf artist's sketch-book, with plain white or green sheets of smooth finish cartridge paper. It can be bought at any good art shop and can be adapted to any desired scheme of field notes, and for a variety of purposes.

As far as bird watching is concerned there is an excellent *Bird-Watcher's Field Pocket-Book* at 3s. 6d., published by Seeley, Service & Co. Ltd., 196 Shaftesbury Avenue, London, W.C.2. It contains, in loose-leaf form, blank outlines of British birds upon which the bird watcher can sketch or write colours, shapes and all other details. There are ample pages for observations and drawings and it can be made as simple or comprehensive as the individual bird watcher wishes. On bird-watching treks using lightweight camping kit it has been used most successfully by Venture Scouts and Ranger Guides, where the leader gave one to each member of the party. Refills may be obtained to fit the binding case, so that individual sections may be altered to suit the prevailing conditions and terrain.

The notes which are most likely to be useful in the field are included in this splendid field-book. They are: Size; Flight; Call; Behaviour; Companions; Nest; Colour; Gait; Song; Food; Sexes alike; Eggs; Observations. Used in conjunction with good field-glasses and *Collins Pocket Guide to British Birds* such a field-book can record a variety of fascinating treks in which bird watching is the prime motive for trekking.

Another useful but more complicated field note-book is entitled *A Nature Record Arranged for Five Years*, compiled by Brian Harrison. The publishers are Messrs. L. Reeve & Co. Ltd., Ashford, Kent. With this note-book the observer can enter up field notes for five consecutive years, which has many obvious advantages. It is a practical, effective note-book. But before very long the trek leader will have to decide whether rough notes or a permanent record are to be kept.

Few of the dragon-flies have popular names: Aeshna cyanea *is one of the largest species. A fine male is seen here drying its wings, while the nymphal skin is attached to the reed above it* (L. Hugh Newman).

A barn owl's pellet dissected (B. Melville Nicholas).

If a boy or girl wishes to keep a plain personal note-book on the lines of an artist's rough sketch-book, I think it is important to have the field notes *exactly as they are made in the field*, with rain spots and so on left on. A practical field book of this kind is much more valuable and authentic than a fair copy made at home with all kinds of trimmings that turn it into an artistic job but not always a true nature log or diary. There is something worth preserving in the actual field note written hastily on a corner of a page as one climbs over a stile. The value of it is seen in the passing years when one remembers the exact circumstances under which the note was made.

A light waterproof case can easily be made or adapted at home for all field note-books, possibly with a "Perspex" cover.

*   *   *

Before long young bird watchers will want to tackle something more advanced than simple recording of birds and nests seen, with relevant data about each one. We can improve our knowledge of bird song and bird calls by listening to several excellent Nature records, including the first-class recordings of Ludwig Koch, which have given many young bird watchers much joy and pleasure. Television programmes, especially on B.B.C. 2 channel, are sometimes valuable.

Modern recordings include an outstanding set of three EP records with a descriptive booklet, entitled *Bird Recognition: An Aural Index* recorded by Victor C. Lewis. This is a completely new series of the songs and calls of 47 British birds and the set can be obtained direct from the British Trust for Ornithology, Beech Grove, Tring, Hertfordshire for £5 0s. 9d. (1970), including postage. Volume I of this attractive set deals with *Birds of Farm and Garden*, Volume II *Birds of Heaths, Commons, Field and Hedgerows*, and Volume III *Birds of Woodland, Copse and Wet Habitat*.

Other publications of the B.T.O. include some excellent Field Guides on binoculars and telescopes, nest-boxes, the treatment of sick and wounded birds, identification for bird ringers and a guide to the moult of British birds; there are also

G

Field Lists of British and European birds. All these varied publications are priced very modestly, with reductions for quantities for Youth Groups.

The most exciting activity of the B.T.O. at the present time is the preparation of an ornithological atlas of Great Britain and Ireland. It will have immense value as a contemporary record of bird distribution and as a baseline for future studies in 25 to 50 years' time. The period of climatic deterioration in Britain which began about 1890 and continued to the 'thirties of this century (and seems to be further continuing!) has resulted in great changes in the distribution of bird species in North-Western Europe. Other factors which affect the pattern of bird distribution include the pressure on bird habitats caused by the continual growth of population, pollution in various forms, changes in farming practice, the development of fisheries and forestry, and population shifts into the many new towns.

As populations of more bird species diminish they become more vulnerable to change, the disturbance of their habitats, and the sheer human pressure as the countryside is used more and more for leisure. During the period from 1970 to about 2020 changes in the number and distribution of birds are as likely to be influenced by pressures from the human environment as by climate. So an Atlas of Bird Distribution in our countryside made around 1970 has a very valuable place in the Conservation of natural resources. Full details of this remarkable project can be found in the regular bulletins known as *BTO News* published by the British Trust for Ornithology.

I would suggest these ideas for bird-watching treks, using lightweight camping, hostelling or canoeing:

> Bird Research, especially feeding habits
> Roosting habits
> Pellets
> Nesting habits
> Migration

Bird Research can be done by absolute amateurs. There is still so much to know and learn about British birds. An article by a boy of sixteen in *British Birds* on the feeding habits of jays in Essex was a remarkable instance of what can be done by young people. His systematic watching of jays collecting acorns in Hainault Forest over a period of two months became the chief source of information on the subject! There is tremendous scope for similar research into the feeding habits of all birds by young people on trek.

I remember a November trek in Hertfordshire. At first it was thought the persistent movement under leaves on the edge of a wood was made by an animal. (A rabbit?) Then a black head appeared. The "rabbit" was a male blackbird eating windfall pears which had dropped in October and never been collected. Leaves had covered them, but the blackbird was not averse to burying himself to get at them. Subsequent observation showed that blackbirds made a daily search for windfall pears as late as December, and in fact until there were no pears left. They would eat a pear for an hour or more at a time, usually in the afternoon between 2 p.m. and 4 p.m.

In November the green woodpecker, hunting alone in open green fields, is another interesting feeding study. Why does he forage so persistently along the edge of flower beds, and in the damp ditch by the side of the lane? He can be found there at all hours of daylight in November.

Roosting Habits. We cannot escape the starlings who roost by the thousand every night on London's tall buildings and also in many other cities and towns, from Manchester to Barnsley. As a bird the starling is very much in the limelight. But there are many much more interesting birds and we know very little indeed about their roosting habits. I have very few details of roost watching on trek by young people, but the British Trust for Ornithology, has made appeals for more observers to watch small and solitary roosts. The address of the Trust is Beech Grove, Tring, Hertfordshire. The bird organization that caters especially for young people is the Junior Bird Recorders' Club, The Lodge, Sandy, Bedfordshire. It is run by the energetic Royal Society for the Protection of Birds and is a lively section. The R.S.P.B.'s valuable journal is called *Bird Notes and News*.

Pellets. One of the most interesting camping treks I ever took part in was a search for owl pellets. We recorded where we found them on One-inch and Six-inch maps, and with the help of an expert naturalist dissected them to find fur, feathers, bits of bone and so on, a valuable aid in deciding what the owls were feeding on. Gulls, herons, crows and some small birds, including robins, cast pellets, and there is scope for some really first-class treks to find and record them. Pellets are made by the bird from food which is not digested or excreted.

The well-known naturalist Maxwell Knight, whose delightful book, *The Young Field Naturalist's Guide* (Bell), I recommend to all young people on Nature treks, advises pellet searchers to look around known nests and the base of isolated tree-stumps or posts used by birds of prey for preening feathers and disgorging pellets, but they may also be found on moors and open country.

Young people on trek are not likely to carry dissecting needles and other equipment of the field naturalist. We used to dissect owl pellets with ordinary nail tweezers and razor blades, after leaving them in soak overnight. A folded piece of white blotting-paper or muslin can be used for the dissecting "operation". Some naturalists keep displays of bird pellets and mount the contents of dissected pellets on white boards, but it is not, apparently, an easy matter to preserve them for an indefinite length of time.

There is a great deal of research work to be done on bird pellets. No one knows why some birds eject them and not others, nor is it known for certain how the birds actually form them prior to ejection or disgorging. Here then is a subject well worth studying by any trekking party of young people.

Nesting Habits always interest young people and there is still much work to be done. A boy discovered jays nesting in a tree-trunk only five feet from the ground, a very rare and quite unusual occurrence, especially as it was close to a footpath. In 1967 I found blackbirds nesting on the ground in thick ivy close to the edge of a stream with high banks. The birds always approached the nest by flying along the stream bed below nest level!

We are familiar with the unusual nesting habit of garden birds, who will build nests in old kettles, pots and pans, rolls of wire netting, saddle-bags and tool-bags hanging in a shed.

A useful and amusing activity is to study nesting habits of field birds and to place artificial aids to good nesting in odd and unfamiliar places. For instance, small discarded teapots (or defective ones can be picked up very cheaply) make excellent nest boxes. Collect half a dozen or so of the brown earthenware kind if possible. (Birds prefer dark ones to white or coloured ones, but don't ask me why!) We found a sale of ex-Army surplus stores gave us as many brown earthenware Naafi teapots of the three- or four-cup size as we wanted at 2d. each. Discard the lid, and the handle if wished. The pot can then be placed in a fork of any tree or bush, spout downwards and slightly tilting forwards to give as much protection from rain as possible. In fact the opening can be improved by blocking it for about two-thirds its area with a piece of three-ply. The spout will result in good draining if rain does get into the pot; wooden nest boxes often get water-logged or sodden in wet weather and are then quickly deserted by the birds, but they will not desert a homely teapot once possession has been taken.

With these teapot nest-boxes we lured tits away from garden peas with great success by erecting them in a nearby spinney in early summer, and putting a mixture or mash of table scraps, bird-seed, oatmeal, flower seeds, and grass-seeds with margarine or dripping inside the pot, which was placed in a tree fork some seven or eight feet above the ground. Before long robins, hedge-sparrows and even a wren had also found the teapot and decided the contents were good.

The next step was obvious. The teapots were used as nesting sites the following season and continued to be used each spring.

An interesting point is that the pots, provided they are of dark colour, may be taken up as sites in open country as well. We carried pots on trek and put them in earth banks of little-used narrow country lanes well covered with natural growth. We also stuck them in low thick bushes on fell and moor, and on the ground itself in sandy open common near the sea, and on a Lakeland fell. On one occasion a rabbit pop-hole was blocked with one. No matter where we used these teapot nest boxes they were invariably accepted as nesting sites by a variety of common birds, especially if placed in a secluded spot with the opening facing East.

The positions can be located on One-inch or Six-inch maps, and then checked on at one-month intervals. We delegated two young people to one teapot, as far as personal responsibility was concerned, and the results have been well worth the time and trouble.

In Germany bird watchers have the delightful habit of putting wooden nest boxes on trees in all parts of their forests. On one sunny March morning I found a German naturalist setting out for a week-end camp in the Weser Valley with twenty-four home-made nest boxes in his capacious rucksack. He was going to nail them all on trees before he came home. He told me he did this regularly every spring. To encourage young people in this habit the Germans make miniature nest boxes for hanging on the wall in their bedrooms. One hangs in my dining-room as a reminder of this delightful custom.

Migration, and the study of the breeding cycles, invariably make a strong appeal to young people who develop a real interest in bird watching. Richard Fitter believes migration watching is rapidly becoming one of the most exciting of all aspects of bird watching, even if we cannot all visit the famous migration stations and bird observatories at Blakeney Point, Norfolk, or Dungeness, Kent, or Fair Isle between Shetland and Orkney. Migration, indeed, can be watched by trekking parties almost everywhere in Britain.

We can go to some suitable vantage point in October and watch several flocks of skylarks or meadow pipits moving south. Where do they go? What routes do they take? How long do they spend on their long journeys south? Do they rest awhile?

All bird watchers can learn about bird-ringing and how birds are ringed, each ring being stamped with a serial number, and bearing an address to which a report may sometime be sent. Information can be collected from wide sources in this way, and young people can take part in bird-ringing if they are reliable and responsible in their work.

A bird which is ringed is truly carrying its own identity card, and some of the stories of migration are almost unbelievable. Manx shearwaters were ringed at Skokholm, an island off Pembrokeshire, and the rings were recovered 5,000 miles away in South America. One bird, it is reliably stated, covered this astounding distance in 81 days. Another shearwater released in Boston, U.S.A., returned to Skokholm in 12½ days, the distance involved being 3,000 miles. More shearwaters were released in unfamiliar terrain at Venice and in the Alps, and they still returned to Skokholm.

Kittiwakes, too, have been recovered from Newfoundland. They were ringed in the Farne Islands, off the Northumberland coast. A tern, ringed in Denmark, was recovered in the West Indies less than three months later. Since young people, used to incredible performances in the air by human beings, will surely ask for the record flight known to be covered by birds we must have the answer! I have read a report stating that a young Arctic tern was ringed and released in Western Greenland. Some fourteen weeks later it was recovered in Natal in South Africa. The tern had covered some 11,500 miles. Truly bird-migration is a fascinating study for all who camp and trek.

FURTHER READING

The monthly journal *British Birds*, published by Messrs, H. F. and G. Witherby Ltd., 61 Watling Street, London. E.C.4

Shorelines—C. F. Tunnicliffe (Collins)

The Handbook of British Birds—(Witherby, 5 vols.)

The Popular Handbook of British Birds—(Witherby)

Collins Pocket Guide to British Birds—Richard Fitter

Collins Guide to Bird Watching—R. S. R. Fitter

Collins Pocket Guide to Nests and Eggs—R. S. R. Fitter

Birds of Town and Village—Richard Fitter (Collins)

The Hamlyn Guide to British and European Birds—Bertel Bruun, Arthur Singer and Bruce Campbell (Hamlyn, 1970)

A Field Guide to the Birds of Britain and Europe—Roger Peterson, Guy Mountfort and P. A. D. Hollom (Collins)

Birds of Britain—J. D. Macdonald (Bell)

Regional Guide to the Birds of Scotland—Kenneth Richmond (Constable)

Watching Birds—James Fisher (Collins)

Finding Nests—Bruce Campbell (Collins)

Bird Recognition (I and II)—James Fisher (Penguin)

Mountain Birds—R. A. H. Coombes (Penguin)

The Young Field Naturalist's Guide—Maxwell Knight (Bell)

CHAPTER 8

Plaster Casting

WINTER is excellent for all kinds of outdoor work, from cutting beech logs to make seats for a log cabin, Scout Group or youth club headquarters, to making surveys of local streams and footpaths. We cannot go far in winter before we become acutely aware of animals and birds even if we cannot see them. Their tracks are everywhere, on the verges of muddy lanes, the edge of ponds and banks of streams, and across a stretch of ploughed land or the prepared sand-pit which every Scout Section can build in the grounds of its own headquarters and use for a variety of practical training in tracking, from staging "mock" accidents to waiting for natural bird tracks.

Animals and bird tracks are well worth studying because they tell us so much about the creatures that made them, and what they were doing at the time. Baden-Powell taught us the value of sound deduction from natural tracks; it was the basis of much of his brilliant training methods in observation. Around or near the tracks we can find nuts, shells, seeds, skins, fur and feather and it will then be fairly easy for the skilled observer to decide what was eaten, when and by whom, or by what!

These tracks are especially clear and easy to interpret when clean, hard snow is on the ground. We can take our young people to the nearest river, stream or pond, or stretch of woodland, and try and identify the tracks we find—rabbit, squirrel, rat, farm cats and dogs, fox, badger. . . Good tracks are worth keeping in more permanent form. They *can* be photographed, but such photography needs the eye and camera of the expert and I have never yet seen satisfactory prints taken of snow tracks by amateurs. Another idea is to sketch them in pencil, which is good practice for logbook decoration, providing the sketches are always in the right proportion.

A useful and quite original idea is to mark the tracks (say, of a rabbit running over hard snow) accurately with a large sheet of tissue paper, or thin paper of any kind, using a piece of charcoal or a very soft pencil. For the purpose the paper may be actually placed over the tracks if the snow is hard enough. The paper is then taken to the headquarters or clubroom of the Scout Section or youth group concerned and the actual tracks transferred to the wall, say at chest height. The tracks may then be painted according to the general decorating scheme followed, e.g. black or dark brown tracks on a plain cream distempered background, or white painted tracks on a plain wooden wall. There are endless variations of this decorative idea, especially if plaster casts are hung or placed on the walls as well.

*　　　*　　　*

In any lane in the vicinity of a mixed farm in winter we can find excellent tracks and we can start making plaster casts of them when the snow has disappeared. Beginners can start with a pony or cow or dog track, looking for a firm track on the verge of the farm lane where the mud is not slushy. First of all we must put a "collar" of thin but tough cardboard round the print. We can make these collars in advance from lengths of pliable cardboard about 12 in. to 15 in. long and 2 in. to 4 in. wide, glueing the edges carefully. If we like we can clip the ends together with paper clips, but glued collars are more satisfactory in practice.

The cast is made of plaster-of-paris which we can buy at any builders' merchants or decorator's supply stores. But if we want to make a specially good plaster cast we get some dental plaster at a chemist's shop: it is much more expensive but very much finer in texture and gives better casts. Carry the plaster around in a tin with a tight-fitting lid and do not let it get damp at any time. Also mark the contents clearly on the container as we do not want it mixed up with our food—a mistake easily made. Carry a suitable tin to mix the plaster paste in and get

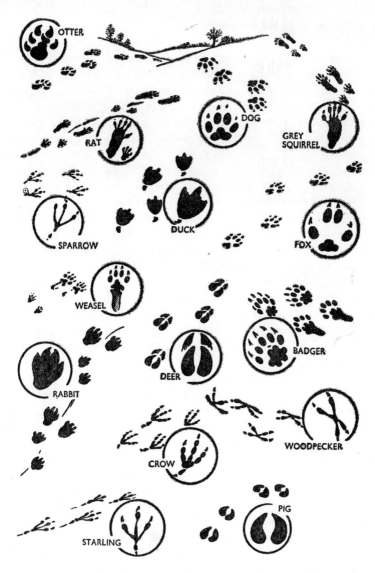

Some British animal and bird tracks which can be sketched in note-books or photographed, or from which plaster casts may be taken

water from the nearest stream or house. At times we may have to carry a bottle of water with us. When we have mixed the plaster to a smooth paste so that there are no lumps in it we tap the sides of the tin to get rid of bubbles. Plaster is used as fresh as possible because air spoils it and if exposed for long it will, of course, harden and become useless. Don't make too much plaster at any one time but just enough to fill the cardboard collar. With practice we can gauge the right amount very quickly.

Just before we pour our plaster into the collar we remove any leaves or twigs from the print. They will spoil it otherwise. Then we pour on the plaster carefully. Let it set as hard as possible. It will do so in a very short time. Then we gently remove the collar and any adhering earth and take the cast home, where we wash it carefully in warm water, removing any mud with a soft brush.

It is real fun to make a collection of such casts to decorate the walls of a headquarters. Write the date on the back of the cast in pencil or Indian ink, or scratch it on with a pin just before the plaster sets in the collar. Paint casts with a hard gloss paint or leave them just as they are. Decorate them in any way, or merely paint them with shellac to make permanent decorations for the home. We can give them away as presents, or make them into book-ends, using a wooden mounting, or wall plaques with very little trouble. If we want to hang them on walls we put a loop of soft wire or string or white tape in the plaster before it sets hard.

Soon we will want to do something better than taking casts of tracks made by the commoner birds and cows, horses, ponies and pigs. We then find it exciting to search on trek for fox, deer and badger tracks and the lesser-known birds along the banks of streams and the seashore.

Casts improve in quality as we make many more of them. Sometimes the plaster cracks or breaks and we have to learn by trial and error the right texture of our plaster mix. To strengthen the cast, and make it more permanent, we can put some hair, or fine wire, or string, or even match-sticks, into the mix. Some cast makers make use of powdered alum or mercerized wax as "strengtheners" but whatever we do we never put salt into the mix, because it makes the cast brittle.

All this casting of tracks (and tree leaves can be cast in the same way) can be tried out in early spring, so that in late spring and summer we know the technique really well.

It is a good plan to "adopt" a stream or pond and get to know it at all seasons of the year, making casts whenever we find something new.

* * *

There are some useful tips worth keeping in mind if we are casting regularly on trek, or in camp. It is a great temptation, particularly with young people, to take too many casts, especially imperfect ones, and there can be plenty of those! We can use up far too much valuable time (valuable in the sense of the number of hours of daylight) and plaster on imperfect or damaged tracks. We need, therefore, a selective method of approach. If our tracking is good we can follow an animal trail down a slope, across a lane and stream, along the edge of a ploughed field and so on until at last we find a really good track without blemish. Streams, ponds and the mudbanks of rivers seem to give the greatest variety of tracks but we are just as likely to find a good track on a sandy heath or common. It means a constant watch for good "trails", and the work is good training in observation.

Before we pour the prepared plaster into our cardboard collar we can, if we wish, smear the inside edge lightly with vaseline to make it easier to withdraw the cast when it is set. If we have no vaseline with us margarine or dripping will do quite well.

One reason for suggesting to young people that they should be selective in their choice of animal and bird casts is that casts are heavy and will soon be a burden in the rucksack. If we carry half a dozen or a dozen casts in the rucksack very far on any kind of day we might soon have dark thoughts about the value of casting! One "trick of the trade" is to wrap up the cast when set hard in newspaper (even with earth still adhering) and post it home in a cardboard box that may have brought a stock of food or chocolate or spare clothing to a Post Office on our route. If we change, and post home soiled clothing to avoid carrying it, we can send casts at the same time. It all helps to save weight when trekking.

In time the skilled caster may not take more than one or two good casts on any one trek. He knows what he wants for his collection and can well afford to leave many good, but commonplace, tracks alone.

Casting is always fun, because young people see something quickly for their efforts, something which they can take home and put in a place of honour in their classroom or in their own room at home. It is neither difficult nor complicated, and is a perfect outdoor activity for camping and hostelling treks.

FURTHER READING

Tracks, Trails and Signs—Fred J. Speakman (Bell)

Tracks—E. A. R. Ennion and M. Tinbergen (Oxford University Press)

Wild Animals of the British Isles—Dr. Maurice Burton (Warne)

Four further titles by Fred J. Speakman, all published by Bell, are of value to animal and bird watchers interested in tracks. They are: *A Poacher's Tale* (1960), *A Keeper's Tale* (1962), *Forest by Night* (1962) and *Out of the Wild* (1967).

Serve by Conserving—Jack Cox (UNESCO/Arco)

CHAPTER 9

Pond Life Study

WHEN we look at the calm surface of a small lake or a country pond on a lightweight camping or youth hostelling trek we might not think that there was a great deal of life there to study. But the quiet appearance is deceptive. Most ponds are *swarming* with living creatures of a great many different kinds, from the very lowest forms of animals to highly specialized members of the insect group, fish and amphibians.

The study of pond life is a very large and enthralling subject and if we want to specialize in this fascinating branch of natural history we must be prepared to spend many seasons of lightweight camping on "pond work" alone. We shall probably enjoy it very much and make many unexpected discoveries, for a pond is a sort of treasure chest. We never know what we shall find next!

We shall not need a lot of equipment in our rucksacks but an essential tool is a strong dredging net of fine mesh with a firm frame which will not bend or break when we scoop about among weeds and in the mud. This will be suitable for capturing all the larger water creatures but if we want to learn about the really small ones as well we shall have to make, or buy, a special kind of net with a cylindrical metal or glass vessel at the bottom so that we can bring up samples of water from various depths without losing the tiny creatures it contains through the mesh. We shall, of course, also need glass jars or metal tins in which to bring home our "captures" and if we really wish to study the various water inhabitants at close quarters (and that is the only way in which we *can* really learn anything about them at first hand) we must have some roomy aquarium tanks in which to keep them for daily observation.

The two pond creatures which almost every boy or girl has tried to rear at some time or other are frogs and newts, but it is not quite such an easy matter as we may think. Of the thousands of tadpoles which are taken home in jam jars every spring very few indeed ever become frogs. Tadpoles cannot be reared in a jam jar filled with tap water. They must be kept in quite a large container, either a tank or a big bowl filled with *pond water*, and there should be a good layer of soil or pond mud at the bottom with plenty of water weeds to keep the water well aerated. To begin with the tadpoles will feed on microscopic creatures called *infusoria*. These occur naturally in pond water but we can also make a culture of them and feed this to the tadpoles at intervals. All this simple field work we can discuss on trek, while studying pond life at first hand.

The simplest way to breed *infusoria* is to put a handful of hay or dry grass in a jam jar, fill it with water and stand it in the sun. After two or three days the water becomes discoloured. This indicates that the *infusoria* have begun to increase, and in another day or so we can pour some of this water into the tank where we keep the tadpoles. A culture like this will not keep fresh for more than a few days, so twice a week we can start a new one.

As the tadpoles grow they will need a more substantial diet and a good way of feeding them is to lower a small piece of fish or meat on a string into the water for about half an hour at a time, and let them suck at this. If we have a thick enough layer of pond mud at the bottom of our tank the tadpoles will find plenty of organic nourishment here, provided we are not trying to rear too many at a time. It is better to keep only half a dozen than to crowd the tank with a large number which will almost certainly die, however careful we may be.

When the tadpoles begin to grow legs and come up to the surface frequently to fill their newly developed lungs with air, it is time to provide them with pieces of cork mat, or flat bits of wood, floating on the water so that they can cling on and crawl up when they are ready. If our tank is large enough we can probably arrange a sort of island at one end and here the

Geological mapping in progress in the Pen-y-Ghent area of North York-shire. This magnificent terrain may be used for many types of field studies (A. Schärer). (Below) mounting bark rubbings taken on a field study course on trees (G. R. Swift).

Guides learn to sail (John Warburton).

young frogs will gather. Baby frogs are even more difficult to rear than tadpoles and it is best to give them their freedom at this stage. The interesting metamorphosis is now over and their subsequent development is just a matter of growing larger. The first of all outdoor treks, with pond life as a *motif*, is worth devoting to tadpoles!

Newts are the most attractive and fascinating of all pond creatures especially in the spring, when the males are so very colourful in their courting dress. We have three species in Britain, the common or smooth newt, the large crested newt which we may not find so easily, and the small palmated newt. Newts can be taken home and kept quite successfully in an aquarium or vivarium. There can be an island for them to cling to, and they must feed regularly. Newts are carnivorous and need things like freshwater shrimps, worms and tadpoles in quite large quantities. They will also eat thin strips of raw beef, or horse meat, obtainable from pet shops.

When the courtship period is over the females lay their eggs carefully folded between leaves of water weeds. The adult newts should not be allowed to stay in the same tank as their offspring or they will quickly eat them all. Young newts are not unlike tadpoles at first and can be fed in the same way on *infusoria*. As they grow they will need water fleas, bloodworms, freshwater shrimps, mosquito larvae and small earthworms. Unless they are given flesh food they will attack each other. When all four legs have developed the young newts leave the water; then we must provide moss, grass and stones in which they can hide.

The close study of freshwater fish is rather too difficult for most young people to undertake and unless we have a pond in a garden where we can place the fish and watch them we shall find it impossible to observe them closely. Young specimens can be kept in ordinary aquarium tanks and if we catch any small fish, either when angling or in our dredge net, it is well worth while to try and keep them at least for a time. A young pike has been kept in an accumulator jar; it seemed perfectly healthy and content and was well fed on animal food. Small perch can be treated in the same way and young dace, roach and

H

rudd are all suitable for an aquarium. The Miller's Thumb is an interesting little fish and if we manage to capture a pair and put them together in a fairly large tank with a good layer of gravel at the bottom they may very well breed in the spring. The male stands guard over the eggs and young fry, and defends them against all enemies. It is fun to watch how he changes colour when he becomes angry or frightened and how both he and his mate can blend in with their background. The Miller's Thumb will grow quite tame and learn to take food from the hand. This fish needs a mixed diet of flesh food.

Another small pond fish specially well suited to an aquarium is the Stickleback and like the Miller's Thumb it is always interesting to watch. During the breeding season the male has a fiery red belly and is emerald green and azure blue above. The female fish merely lays her eggs and then loses all interest in her progeny, while the male undertakes all the duties of a parent. First of all he builds a nest among the weeds. When it is filled with eggs he stands guard outside, sending streams of fresh water over the eggs by movements of his tail and fins. When the fry hatch he herds them together and defends them until they can begin to look after themselves. Sticklebacks are carnivorous and will eat water fleas, worms, shrimps and tadpoles. The mature males usually die soon after their families are reared. Never put two males in the same tank. They attack each other and fight so fiercely that very often both die of their wounds.

In almost every pond we can find quite a number of insects which are easy to observe. Among them are the two largest water beetles, the carnivorous Great Water Diver, sometimes called the Water Tiger, and the vegetarian Silver Water Beetle. The former is by far the more common insect. It is nearly an inch and a half long and has a yellow margin round its body. The females usually have longitudinal grooves on their wing cases. It is not difficult to keep these beetles in captivity provided they have plenty of live food, freshwater shrimps, worms, caddis grubs, tadpoles and so on. It is as well to have a cover over the tank as the Great Diver can fly, and might take to the wing one night and disappear. Another thing to remember if we are keeping a pair of these beetles is that they must have the tank to themselves because they will attack and wound even creatures much larger than they are. If we pick them up we should handle them carefully for on the underside of the body there is a sharp two-pronged spine, pointing backwards. In self-defence the beetles will try to drive these weapons into fingers and they can cause quite nasty wounds.

When dredging about in a pond our youth group may catch a Diver larva, an agile long-legged creature with a pair of wicked-looking curved jaws. Like their parents, these larvae are carnivorous, feeding at first on water fleas and gradually attacking larger and larger prey and sucking the juices from their bodies with their hollow jaws. The larva of the Silver Water Beetle is rather similar but more sluggish and, instead of the curved jaws, it has powerful biting mandibles. Its chief food is freshwater snails. Both these beetle larvae pupate on dry land close to the water's edge so we must provide an island for them when they are full grown. The adult Silver Water Beetle is a fairly peaceful creature and normally feeds on water weeds but occasionally it will attack some smaller insect.

The dragon-fly larvae mentioned in Chapter 12 are also, of course, carnivorous. We are almost certain to capture some of these and it is very interesting to keep them and watch the change from nymph to dragon-fly. If we make notes and drawings of the different kinds at various stages of their development we can in time learn to recognize the nymphs so that we shall know what kind of dragon-fly or damsel-fly they will eventually become.

Two curious water insects which we may also come across are the water scorpion and the water stick insect. They belong to the bug family, and are closely related to each other although they look very different. Both are rather sluggish creatures and catch their prey by lying in wait among weeds and muddy rubbish until some likely victim comes within striking distance. The water scorpion is a rather ugly, flat, mud-coloured insect with a long appendage at the end of its body. This is not a sting but a kind of "snork" or breathing tube. It is a very useful device and enables the creature to lie hidden in the mud just below the surface of the water in shallow places and get its air supply without having to move. Another extraordinary thing about the water scorpion is that if we lift up its wing cases we discover underneath them a pair of delicate membraneous wings with purple veins and a body striped in red and black, but strangely enough it is unable to fly.

The water scorpion is in no way related to the real scorpion, but its front legs, shaped like claws, look very like the claws of a scorpion. With the aid of these the insect grips and holds its prey. The water stick insect has forelegs made on a similar pattern, but rather more sickle-shaped and hinged in such a way that they can fold up like a penknife. Although it normally moves very slowly, walking laboriously through the water on its long thin legs, it can move these "arms" with lightning speed and strike and hold a victim before the creature has any chance of getting away. In looks it resembles nothing so much as a piece of sodden straw. One would not think that such an attenuated creature would need a great deal of food. But the water stick insect is always hungry and if we keep one in our aquarium it must be well supplied with a variety of live food. Like the water scorpion it has wings, but seldom flies.

The water boatmen are typical pond dwellers, also classified as bugs. There are many different species but we can easily distinguish the two main groups by the way they swim. Those belonging to the family *Corixidae* swim in a normal position with their backs towards the surface of the water while the *Notonectidae* swim upside down. There are other differences as well. The genus *Corixa* takes in air at the junction between head and thorax and swims with both the second and third pair of legs which are of about equal length. *Notonecta* on the other hand brings the tip of its hind body to the surface for breathing and it is the third pair of legs which act mainly as "oars". The body of this bug is shaped very much like a boat, flat on the abdominal surface and keeled on the back. *Notonecta* is carnivorous and will attack all kinds of creatures including fishes and is quite capable of giving a nasty prick with its long snout, while *Corixa* feeds mainly on the juices of water plants. The males of the *Corixa* have the ability to make a noise, not unlike the chirping of a grasshopper, by rubbing the forelegs against the beak-like proboscis.

While all the insects mentioned so far live right in the water we can also find quite a number on the surface. The pond skaters of the genus *Gerris* are the largest of these. They are quite difficult to capture although we might think at first that it would be the easiest thing in the world. They, too, are bugs, not beetles, and with their long legs outstretched they jerk along on the surface as if they were skating over thin ice. On the underside their bodies are covered in dense hair, like velvet, and this holds so much air that it is impossible for them to get wet and drown. Pond skaters feed on all kinds of little insects which happen to fall into the water such as aphids, small flies, young caterpillars and the like. They can fly quite well and if we keep them in a tank it must be covered or they will very soon escape.

The Whirligig beetles are favourites with most young people, and they well deserve their name. They swim about on the surface at great speed in circles and spirals. Their movements are so rapid that it is difficult to follow them with the eye. On cold dull days they dive down and hide in the mud or shelter among the plants at the edge of the pond, but in sunny weather they become very active. When danger threatens they dive and if they want to fly they crawl up on some water plant, raise their wing cases and set off. These little beetles have very curious eyes, specially adapted for their kind of life. A narrow strip divides the eyes into two separate halves, the upper section being adapted for watching the surroundings above water, while the lower section can peer beneath the surface for any likely prey. The larvae have long narrow bodies and carry thread-like gills on each segment of the abdomen.

The water spider occurs in many districts in the south of England. It prefers clear clean ponds with plenty of insect life. It has a brown body and long hairy legs and can run across the surface of the water and dive down below and swim as well. Their prey is usually caught below water and then either brought to the surface or into the nest before it is devoured. The water spider constructs a remarkable nest under water, suspended among weeds. First of all it spins a close mat of silk and then proceeds to carry down bubbles of air from the surface between its hind legs. These bubbles are released beneath the web, rise up, and are caught in the mesh, and gradually as the web fills with air it assumes the shape of a narrow dome or bell. The female spider fixes her cocoons of eggs to the ceiling of her diving bell, and the young spiders leave this shelter soon after they have hatched. An unusual thing about the water spider is that the male is larger than the female and the pairs live quite amicably together, building their nests close beside each other, joined by a "covered way" of silk. They hibernate in the winter, either inside their bells which have been sealed with a door of silk, or in empty shells, lined with silk and carefully closed at the entrance.

There is also another spider, called the Raft Spider, which a boy or girl may find running about on the water surface. It is common in the Fen district. This spider does not swim or dive but merely hunts on the water or around the margins. It is bright brown in colour, edged with a conspicuous streak of bright yellow.

The freshwater mites are allied to the spiders and there are as many as 250 different kinds found in Britain. They vary a great deal in shape but most of them are richly coloured. They can easily be seen with the naked eye. One of the commonest kinds is scarlet and almost globular in shape with symmetrical dark blotches. The small light-red eggs are laid in neat rows on the under side of water-lily leaves or on stones. The larvae attach themselves as parasites to water beetles and other aquatic insects.

In all ponds and pools of any size the water fleas play a most important part in the balance of life because they are the basic food of all the other carnivorous creatures. These minute animals are not insects but crustaceans, and their rapid increase under favourable weather conditions is, in many ways, similar to the propagation of aphids on dry land. Several generations of females follow each other in quick succession, in some cases right through the summer, and as each individual takes only about a week to mature they increase in numbers amazingly fast. Then a generation of males appears, followed again either by a succession of females or by a resting period in the egg stage, which in some species lasts all the winter. Water fleas are about the same size as ordinary fleas and either light brown, reddish or completely colourless and transparent. They move about with a jerky jumping motion.

In studying pond life young people can preserve the various creatures for a collection by setting and drying, or by keeping them in formalin or spirit. Various methods of dealing with different insects are detailed in Chapter 12. The most important thing however is to observe closely individual insects under conditions which are as natural as possible, making accurate notes about their behaviour. In this book it is only possible to mention very briefly a few of the many different things we may expect to find in lake, pond or pool when we are on trek, and if we really want to make a serious study of this subject we should read a comprehensive specialist book about it.

FURTHER READING

The Freshwater Life—John Clegg (Warne)
Freshwater Microscopy—W. J. Garnett (Constable)
The Fishes of the British Isles—J. Travis Jenkins (Warne)
Shell Life—Edward Step: Revised by A. Laurence Wells (Warne)

These books also apply to Chapter 10 on Stream Life Study

CHAPTER 10

Stream and River Study

SLOW-MOVING lowland streams such as we often find on exploring treks often contain many creatures which we can also find in ponds and pools, but there are a number of water dwellers which prefer a slight current and usually breed in rivers and streams rather than in still water.

The Crayfish, our largest freshwater crustacean, is one of these and it is fairly common all over the country south of Lancashire. A full-grown crayfish has a body about four inches long from head to tail and in the males the claws are almost as long again. In the female the claws are much shorter and weaker. A crayfish looks exactly like a miniature lobster and is the same dark colour. Like its larger relative it turns scarlet when boiled. It has a tremendous appetite and will consume almost anything that is edible, whether it be vegetable or flesh food, and it appears to relish putrid meat or fish in particular.

Crayfish are more or less nocturnal in their habits although we sometimes see them moving about in the day-time, but usually they stay hidden in hollows under stones or in the river bank until dusk. Then they come out and begin to prowl about and that is the time when we can most easily capture them. They are attracted by bright lights shining near the water. If we camp near a placid stream we can bait a trap or even an old sieve standing in the water, and then shine a light near it. We are almost certain to catch a crayfish or two—provided they live in that stream. A piece of fish, meat, or rabbit paunch will be a suitable bait and while we are waiting for the crayfish to arrive we must keep quiet. If we use a sieve it must have a rope or strong string attached to it in such a way that we can pull it straight out of the water without tipping it. Years ago crayfish were often caught for food in Britain but now one seldom hears of anyone fishing for them, although on the Continent they are highly prized as a table delicacy. Continental campers often eat them for supper!

A crayfish is quite an interesting animal to take home to watch in an aquarium, but it needs a really large tank and the water has to be aerated by a small electric pump which blows bubbles through a pipe. It is useless to plant weeds because the crayfish will uproot them and tear them to pieces. Make a hiding-place with a few large stones in one corner and feed the animal on a mixture of sliced vegetables, freshwater snails, insects, tadpoles, fish roe, fish and meat. When it is growing rapidly a crayfish has to change its shell at intervals. This is quite a difficult process and may take several days. After the shell has been cast it is quite often eaten to provide lime salts to harden the new shell, which at first is quite soft and light in colour. The crayfish will expand very rapidly during the first few days after the old shell has been cast while the new covering is still flexible and able to stretch.

The freshwater shrimps mentioned in Chapter 9 as a suitable food for fish and carnivorous insects occur abundantly in slow streams and rivers. We can often find them among the stalks of freshwater cress. Even when we buy the bunches from the greengrocer's shop the shrimps are usually still alive because they have been kept damp. Like the crayfish they are crustaceans but belong to a different family. Their bodies are not so sharply divided into head, thorax and tail and they have no claws. The freshwater shrimp has a curved back and its body is flattened from the sides. It swims in rather a jerky manner, weaving in and out among the water weeds. If we turn up stones or logs lying at the bottom of a stream we shall find dozens of these shrimps congregated underneath them. In colour they are pale buff or grey-buff and they eat both vegetable and animal food.

During very cold winter weather the freshwater shrimps dig themselves down into the sand or mud at the bottom of the stream until the temperature rises again. The breeding season is in the spring, and the females carry their eggs in pockets at the base of their legs. Even after hatching the young shrimps remain with their parent for a time, sheltering between her numerous legs!

The Water Slaters are very like the freshwater shrimps and are closely related to them but instead of having flat sides they are flat above and look rather like woodlice with long feelers.

Among all the stream and river insects the Mayflies are in a class by themselves and, as a group, are well worth studying. There are many different kinds. Altogether we have forty-seven different species in the British Isles, and they differ quite a lot from each other both in habits and in size. The mayfly which fishermen call the "dun", and later the "spinner", is the largest kind, measuring an inch and a half across the wings. These insects normally appear in the early summer and then very often in dense swarms. The spectacular "rise of the may-fly", which is such a fascinating thing to watch, means that thousands of these insects have been transformed from under-water nymphs into aerial creatures at the same time. The mayfly has become a symbol of a brief life. Although the nymphs may live in the water for as long as a year the adult insects some-times only last a day and seldom more than three or four.

When the mayfly first emerges from the skin of the nymph it is rather dull in colour and the wings are covered in silky hairs. At this stage it is known as the "dun", and the flight is rather heavy and slow. The "dun" does not fly very far but settles on some water plant or on a leaf on some branch overhanging the stream. If we are spending one day by the river-side we may well notice a dun settling like this. We shall probably have a look at it now and then. Presently we shall begin to wonder when it is going to fly again. If we look really close we may notice that the creature sitting on the leaf is not a live mayfly at all but simply an empty skin.

The mayfly is unique among insects in the way it changes its skin after it has emerged as a fully winged insect. The "dun" is known to scientists as a sub-imago and is not yet the fully mature insect. This has yet to emerge from the skin of the "dun" and the shedding of the entire body covering, including the wings, is a difficult and very delicate operation. In its final form the mayfly or "spinner" is a lighter and more beautiful creature, with a metallic lustre on its dark body and transparent netted wings and three long narrow filaments at the end of the body.

Not until now are the mayflies ready to begin that fascinating dance over the water for which they are so famous. It is the males that begin this dance. In huge swarms they rise and fall rhythmically over the stream, waiting and watching for the females, which join the company a little later. Every female soon finds a mate and together they leave the dancing swarm. Before a day has passed each female will have dropped nearly five thousand eggs into the water. As soon as the future of the race is assured the dancing life of the adult mayflies comes to an end. Quickly they lose strength and fall into the water, where eager fish are waiting to snap them up.

The eggs sink down to the bottom of the stream and there they hatch into nymphs which live in burrows in the mud or in the banks. These burrows are constructed in such a way that they have an opening at each end. The nymphs have six legs, fairly long antennae, three tail filaments and external gills on the hind body. These gills are folded up over the back so as not to rub against the sides of the burrows. By a slight movement of the gills the nymphs keep a constant current of water flowing through their burrows so that they always have a plentiful supply of oxygen.

Not all mayflies are burrow-dwellers and many of the nymphs live quite freely on the bottoms of streams and ditches. We may very well find some when we dredge about with a net. We can always recognize them by their tail filaments, which are either two or three in number, and the fringed gills down each side of the hind body. It is interesting to watch them in a tank or glass jar and especially to observe the movements of the gills. If the water is fresh and full of oxygen the gills only move very slowly, but if the oxygen content is very low (for example if the water has been boiled and then cooled again) the gills begin to move so rapidly that we can hardly see them, except as a blur.

The Sponge Fly is a small aquatic insect which we may come

across as we trek along quiet streams, where it sits on reeds and rushes. It is dark in colour, with smoky transparent wings and flies rather feebly. We must be fairly observant to notice these little flies at all, because they are less than half an inch in wing span. The nymphs are correspondingly tiny and we can only find them inside freshwater sponges, where they live as parasites. The river sponge grows on water plants, or on wood and stones, and if we pull one apart we shall most likely find these nymphs right inside it. When they are full grown they leave the water and spin silken cocoons on some firm foundation above water-level.

The Alder flies are larger but have the same kind of netted transparent wings. They appear in April and May along the banks of slow muddy streams and, like the Sponge flies, they are more often found sitting about in the sun than actively flying. It is fairly easy to find their eggs if we search for them on the leaves of reeds and other water plants. These eggs are brown and are laid close together in little patches which look like brown velvet. As soon as the larvae hatch they allow themselves to drop down into the water.

The nymphs are carnivorous and have large heads with curved jaws and their bodies end in a single, fringed filament. At first glance we might think that they have a great number of legs, but actually they only have the usual three pairs, while the appendages on the hind body are jointed gills. A characteristic habit of these Alder fly nymphs is to move their bodies up and down with a whip-like motion to encourage a fresh flow of water across the gills. Young people can keep them in an aquarium, but they must be fed well on bloodworms, mosquito larvae, freshwater shrimps and water fleas. They complete their growth in one season and towards the spring crawl out of the water and pupate in the earth. This resting stage only lasts a fortnight or so before the adults emerge.

There is a small copper-coloured, or metallic green, beetle known as the Leaf Beetle, which we can often see sunning itself on reeds and other plants along the water's edge. The larvae of these pretty insects live in the water among the roots of plants, specially the water grass *Glyceria aquatica*. Although these larvae have no gills and are therefore compelled to breathe atmospheric air they never come to the surface. Instead, they obtain their supply of oxygen from the roots of the grass by inserting two tail hooks furnished with breathing pores into the spongy tissues, and thus "tapping" the plants' supplies.

Among the lower forms of animal life which we shall find in every river and stream on our treks are the Freshwater Snails. They are very simple creatures to breed in captivity, as they feed on water weeds, and especially on the algae which quickly grow on the glass of a tank standing in a sunny position. They lay their eggs in batches on the side of the tank and here we can easily watch them develop and hatch. The young snails grow quite rapidly and complete their life span in a year or two.

The Freshwater Mussels are much more long-lived. The famous pearl mussel is found in clear and fast-running streams. It has a very interesting life story including a parasitic phase when, soon after hatching from the eggs, the young mussels live for a time attached to the gills of fishes enclosed in small "blisters". Occasionally quite valuable pearls are found inside the shells of these mussels, and the creatures are said to live as long as eighty or a hundred years. We can judge their ages by counting the rings on the shell. Each ring represents a year's growth.

*　　　　*　　　　*

Some field work in recent years in South-East England included the search for the Mitten Crab, a creature which first arrived in Europe from China at the turn of the century.

WHAT TO DO—MORE SPECIALIZED INTERESTS

Bicycle touring along the Pilgrim's Way near Kemsing Youth Hostel, Kent
(Peter Knottley).

Guides learning cliff rescue techniques; (below) *pony trekking across country* (both the Girl Guides' Association).

CHAPTER 11

Butterflies and Moths

THE SIGHT of a fluttering butterfly on a fine summer's day often fires a boy or girl with the desire to record the beautiful insect, and that is very natural. There is no harm in "collecting" butterflies. Except for a few of the rarer species, which are on the protected list and mostly very local. It is important, if we decide to make butterfly collecting the main object of a camping or hostelling trek, to begin with the right apparatus.

The only really satisfactory kind of net is a jointed one that folds up and fits into the coat pocket, and it should have a bag made of *black* mosquito netting. It is much easier to see an insect through the folds of black netting than any other colour. The stick which fits into the brass Y-piece can be used as a walking stick until the "collecting" ground is reached.

Always carry a killing-bottle in each pocket, because if we put two lively insects in a bottle together they are very likely to damage each other's wings; using our bottles alternately greatly diminishes this risk. There is a safe non-poisonous killing-bottle on the market, but many entomologists prefer one which can be made up cheaply and easily by any chemist. It is a good plan to carry a relaxing tin in the rucksack, and when we arrive at the chosen spot, to dump everything in the shade of a bush. We can then make this bush our headquarters, and when the butterflies are dead we can return there and empty them into the relaxing tin. This is by far the best method of securing perfect specimens for a collection. We should make quite sure that all the insects in the killing-bottles are dead before emptying them into the tin, which means they should all have been in there for at least half an hour. Otherwise one or two of the last ones to be caught may revive and cause great havoc by crawling about among the rest of our catch.

A relaxing tin is an essential part of our equipment, for after a short while a dead insect goes completely stiff, and it cannot be mounted on a setting-board until this *rigor mortis*, or stiffness, is broken down. The main ingredients of a relaxing tin are chopped laurel leaves and a chemical to prevent mould forming on the insects enclosed in the tin. Here again it is far better to buy one from an entomological dealer or naturalists' store than to try and concoct our own; there is nothing more disappointing than to discover mould all over the specimens that have taken so much time and trouble to collect. We must also invest in a pair of curved entomological forceps for picking up specimens, remembering never to take hold of them by their wings, but always by the legs.

While on the practical side of butterfly collecting, I would like to pass on to the reader a setting lesson by L. Hugh Newman, the butterfly authority.

"Choose a good steady table to work at and have everything ready before you take the insects from your relaxing tin. You will need a selection of cork setting-boards, a pair of forceps, a setting-needle and a box of mixed pins. Now pick up one of the butterflies carefully with the forceps and lay it on the palm of your right hand. Take hold of the body gently between your left thumb and forefinger and apply a light pressure.

"If the insect is sufficiently relaxed this will cause the wings to open. Choose a pin of suitable size and insert it near the front of the thorax, almost at right angles to the butterfly's body, but sloping just very slightly forwards. Push it down until two-thirds of the pin protrudes on the under side.

"Holding the head of the pin with the forceps you should now fix the insect on the board. This must be done with great care for unless the butterfly is correctly pinned the setting will be a failure. Make certain that the insect is placed right in the centre of the groove and adjust its height so that the wings are at exactly the right level. If you push the butterfly too deep down the wings will 'spring' when it is taken off the board, and an insect set with wings sloping downward looks very bad in the cabinet.

"Now the actual setting can begin. First of all pin down the setting tape on the left-hand side so that the wings cannot move too much while you set the right side. Hold the right tape down with your left hand and coax the wings on this side into position with the aid of the setting-needle, beginning with the forewing. You can do this either by pricking the wing at its thickest point close to the thorax and gently pushing it upwards, or by inserting the needle underneath the wing, near the outer margin.

"You must be very careful not to scratch and mark the wing, or worse still tear holes in it with the needle. Manipulate the hind wing in the same way and the moment when you get it into the correct position bring the tape right down so that it lies taut across the wings and pin it first just below the hind wing and then close to the upper margin of the fore wing. The left side of the insect is set in the same way, but right-handed people find it rather more difficult to do. If the antennae need adjusting fix them into their correct position with pins on either side and finally put two rather wide strips of transparent setting paper over the wings on either side, so that they are almost completely covered. If you are setting a whole board full of insects these tapes are pinned on last of all. When you have filled a board with insects you should not leave it about on the mantelpiece but store it away in a cupboard, as some insects fade quite quickly and there are all sorts of 'pests' that eat set insects, such as mites, the larvae of clothes-moths and 'museum' beetles. I have even found wasps cutting up the bodies of moths on a setting-board and carrying them away to feed their grubs!"

⋆   ⋆   ⋆

So far we have assumed that campers and hostellers are only interested in catching butterflies and moths to form a collection. But it is far more interesting to breed them in captivity, and for this fascinating hobby we shall need rather different apparatus.

The net will be the same, but instead of a killing-bottle we shall need a satchel of pill-boxes and a botanist's collecting tin. The most inexpensive kind of pill-box is the type used by chemists for ointments, but they are not very satisfactory, as they are often rather flimsy and we cannot see the specimen inside when we have successfully boxed it. Boxes with glass bottoms are the best, and can be bought from most entomological dealers in "nests" of six, ranging from an inch to three inches in diameter.

There is a definite technique in boxing an insect which is fluttering in the net. If we are beginners we shall probably find it best to lay the net on the ground, but otherwise we can hold the stick or handle firmly between our legs and fold the bag across the frame so that the butterfly cannot escape. Take out a box and remove the lid. Holding the box in our right hand, we push it into the net and trap the insect, keeping the net taut across the opening of the box so that it cannot flutter out again. Slide the lid down into the bag and manœuvre it on to the box. If we blow gently through the net it will help to keep the insect down in the box during the brief moment when we actually put the lid on.

There is a correct way of catching a butterfly. Distinguished entomologists very seldom run after one, not because they are too old or that it is undignified, but simply because they do not want to frighten the butterflies away. Watch a butterfly on a sunny day. It will flit from flower to flower seeking nectar; when it settles is just the right time to catch it. But do not rush at it; move towards the insect with the net bag held up between the thumb and first finger, and do not let the shadow fall on the feeding butterfly. Approach closer and closer, crouching down if the butterfly is on a flower near the ground. Then, when you are within eighteen inches to two feet of it, smash the net down on top of it, still holding the bag aloft so that the butterfly will rise up into the muslin folds. The same technique can be used if the butterfly settles on a flowering bush, as long as it is not out of reach.

Now if we decide to start breeding butterflies as a result of butterfly treks we shall first of all have to learn to tell the difference between the sexes, for only females are of any use for this purpose. The Blues are easy to tell apart, as in the majority of the species only the males are blue, the females being brown. The Fritillaries vary very little between the sexes, and most difficult of all to distinguish are the Vanessas, which include the Peacock, Red Admiral, and the Small Tortoiseshell.

The best way to tell the sex of a difficult species is to examine its body. This is always much plumper in the female than in the male, and the insect itself is usually rather larger. But the only real test, of course, is to see if it lays eggs!

A female butterfly likes fresh young plants on which to deposit her eggs, and so before we set out on our first collecting trip we must do a little gardening, and pot up some common weeds that the caterpillars, of the kind in which we are interested, will feed on. For example, the family of Browns, which include the Meadow Brown, the Gatekeeper, and the Ringlet, all feed on grass, and so they are very easy to feed; the Vanessas mostly like stinging nettles, and if we wear rubber gloves it is quite easy to transplant some roots of these plants into pots.

The best kind of breeding cage in which to confine butterflies for laying is a round cheese tub which can still be bought from a grocer for about a shilling. Then we must buy enough black mosquito netting, or butter muslin, to cover the top, which can be easily secured by strong string or twine tied round the tub. Gather a bunch of fresh flowers and put them in a bottle or jam jar of water. Place this in the cheese tub with a pot of growing food-plant and the breeding cage is ready for its first occupant. In order to lay, butterflies *must* have warmth and sunshine, so find a sunny corner in the garden sheltered from the wind, or if in a town then find a window facing south. Stand the tub there.

I do not recommend that we start with the Blues, as they must associate with ants to keep healthy. The Browns are not very easy either, as they hibernate as tiny caterpillars and in captivity sometimes die during the winter months. The best butterflies to catch in the spring are Small Tortoiseshells. They are very common; the females lay readily in a tub fitted up as I have described. After a few days, take out the pot of stinging nettles at dusk and look underneath the leaves; if we have been lucky and caught a female there should be a big batch of green eggs all piled on top of each other attached to the underside of a leaf. In about three weeks' time these will hatch into a brood of minute caterpillars which will immediately begin to spin a web and here they will live feeding on the leaves nearby. Soon we shall have to give them cut nettles in a bottle of water, as they grow very fast and eat a tremendous lot of greenstuff. When they are fully grown each caterpillar will attach itself by a silken pad to the top of the muslin, or a nettle stem, and hanging head downwards will cast off its skin for the last time and then change into a chrysalis. We shall only have to wait a week or ten days, according to how warm the weather is, before the first butterflies that we have bred successfully begin to emerge— and what a thrill it is! It may not be as easy as this first time, I need hardly add.

Now we mentioned a botanist's collecting tin as a very useful item for the butterfly breeder. This can be used for carrying sprigs of food-plant if we decide that it is easier to search for the eggs of butterflies instead of trying to get them to lay in captivity. If we walk down a country lane in spring and search the flower heads of the plant called Jack-by-the-hedge (check it against a good wild flower or plant reference book) we can very often find the bright orange eggs of the Orange-tip butterfly. Or we may wish to breed the Brimstone butterfly; in this case we must look on the terminal shoots of the buckthorn bushes in the hedgerows for the yellow eggs these butterflies lay on the leaves.

Buy a good book on butterflies. It will describe all the different food-plants, and what the eggs and the caterpillars look like, and this is really a first essential for the butterfly breeder.

*   *   *

Young people may feel that moths are more interesting to collect than butterflies, and if this is so, expeditions from our tents will mostly start at dusk. The two methods of night collecting are by sugaring tree-trunks or attracting moths to light. Let us suppose then that we have reached a clearing in a local wood and are going to try sugaring for the first time. We shall have with us a satchel filled with pill-boxes, a killing-bottle, our net, forceps, a torch, and the most important item of all, the treacle-pot and brush! Young people love this. We should plan to reach the wood about half an hour before dusk, so that we can smear the first coating of treacle on the tree-trunks before any moth is on the wing, as this gives plenty of time for the rich aroma of the "mixture" to circulate into the surrounding atmosphere.

There are many factors that go to make a perfect sugaring night. Dark nights are preferable to moonlit ones. There should be a faint breeze to carry the scent of our sugaring mixture, and it does not matter at all if there is a slight drizzle as long as the night is warm. Many entomologists have their own special recipe which they think attracts the most moths, but we really cannot beat the old-fashioned one recommended to me by L. Hugh Newman. Take a pint of brown ale and a tin of un-refined or "black" treacle. Thicken it with brown sugar, and slowly bring to the boil. When the concoction has cooled it may be spooned into old treacle tins, but before sealing down the lid pour in a tablespoonfull of sherry or rum, and stir it well in. This is a very special brew!

If we make a round of some twenty trees, painting each one with a patch of sugar about a foot square, this should take us about half an hour. By the time the last one is well coated dusk will have fallen and the moths will be on the wing seeking out the sweet-smelling "bait". If we strike a lucky night our catch can be really amazing! It is a wonderful sight to see the moths crowded round the edge of the sticky black patch. Notice how their wings quiver as they suck up the mixture in evident de-light. Their eyes appear scarlet in the glare of the torch. If we merely want moths for our collection we must have our net ready, and, holding the bag extended, slap the frame against the part of the tree-trunk on which the rarest moths are feeding. The net bag will no doubt get sticky (not to mention aromatic!) but it can be washed easily. If, however, we only want female moths for breeding purposes, it is best to box them straight off the tree-trunk, and with a little experience we shall soon get the knack of it.

In the morning we can examine our catch at leisure and decide which we wish to retain. We may even find that some of the females have already begun to lay eggs round the rim of the box in which they were confined. They will certainly not be as difficult to sex as butterflies, for in many species of moths the males have thick "feathered" antennae, while the females have thread-like or plain ones.

The other way to attract moths by night is by using artificial light. I said that moths do not like moonlit nights, and this is perfectly true. But it is a curious thing that they are irresistibly drawn to a candle, as all young people have noticed, and so it will be realized how far more potent a high-powered electric light beam can be in its attraction. Entomologists now find mercury vapour lamps are even more effective, but, as they are still very expensive, we shall not go into their use now. We can easily prove, however, what a good method light is by stretching a white sheet across a frame just inside a room, and then arranging a powerful electric light bulb behind it. From dusk onwards moths will begin to fly towards the bedroom window, and they can easily be boxed or netted as they flutter up and down the white sheet. Be sure to choose a warm, sultry night for the first attempt at this method of moth trapping, and you will not be disappointed.

There is still one other way to collect moths, especially in the spring and autumn, and this is by visiting the sallow bushes when they are in flower in late March and April, or the ivy blossom in September. Quite large hauls can be taken, and for the collector who wants to breed this method is recommended. To save a great deal of searching take an umbrella and a stout walking stick. All we then need to do is to tap the flowers, and the moths will come tumbling into the "beating tray". By the light of a torch we can select just the ones we want because they "sham death" for quite a time after being knocked down.

I think I can truthfully say this about butterfly and moth collecting. Once a party of young people have made a start they will never have a dull moment wherever they may be. There is no "close season", as many species of moths do not begin to emerge until November and December, and we can always find pupae to dig for beneath trees, or we can search for hibernating caterpillars in the hedgerows if we go on a hostelling trek during the winter months. When spring comes round again such a season of emerging awaits that it almost bewilders one to think of it—the arrival of the migrant butterflies, and the rare hawk moths!

FURTHER READING

Living with Butterflies—L. Hugh Newman (John Baker)
Create a Butterfly Garden—L. Hugh Newman and Moira Savonius (John Baker)
The Complete British Butterflies in Colour—L. Hugh Newman and E. Mansell (Ebury Press and Michael Joseph)

CHAPTER 12

Insects

MOST YOUNG PEOPLE who collect insects choose butterflies and moths, but there is even more scope for collectors among the other orders of insects—in fact much more, because the *Lepidoptera* are only a comparatively small group. Beetles, for example, far outnumber them and there are so many in Britain alone that we can hardly hope to be able to collect them all during a lifetime. They vary in size from the Giant Stag Beetle and the clumsy Oil Beetle to tiny creatures which are almost too small to see clearly with the naked eye. We can find beetles everywhere, indoors as well as outside, flying in the air and swimming in the water and our beetle collecting can go on all the year round. In fact "beetle treks" are always fun.

Beetle collecting entails a lot of searching among moss and leaves, under bark and stones, beneath decaying rubbish and debris of all kinds. It is useful to have a short little hand-rake or fork when we go collecting. Beetles often hide in mole-hills in the winter, and ants' nests also have their own special beetle population. In summer we can find many beetles sitting on flowers, specially on hogweed and hedge parsley, and if we sweep along the ground with a strong net or hold an open umbrella under the branches of a low tree, or a shrub, and beat the foliage with a stick, we are certain to capture many different kinds of beetles which become dislodged and fall down into our "beating tray".

If we come across the body of a dead bird or rabbit on our treks and rambles, there are almost certain to be sexton beetles busily digging beneath it. In the autumn many beetles are attracted to fungi and feed inside the stems, and on the undersides of the caps. Storehouses and barns often yield a good haul of beetles if we search corners and cracks, and move old sacks and rubbish.

For catching water beetles, such as the great Silver Water beetle, or the little Whirligig beetles, we need a small firm net, so that we can scoop about in the mud and among the water weeds. We can make quite an efficient beetle trap by sinking a jam jar to the neck in some likely spot, and baiting it with a piece of fish, or with meat scraps covered with moss. Lodge a stone or tile over the top so that the jar does not become swamped with water when it rains. Many beetles will make their way down and be unable to get out again. Visit the trap every few days and collect the booty.

Don't kill a beetle immediately it is caught. The contents of its abdomen will decay and spoil its colour and appearance. Beetles should be kept alive for a couple of days in a tin in which we have put a little grass on which they will cling. Make some air holes in the lid, if the beetles are large, and do not put a lot of beetles together, as they may damage each other. It is really safest to keep them singly and if they are tiny we can use small glass tubes or test tubes. Entomological dealers usually sell these.

A simple and efficient way of killing small beetles is to put them in a teacup or a mug and pour boiling water over them. They will die instantly, and are then soft and can be set at once. Another method is to use chopped laurel leaves. Gather these in May when they are soft and bright green, and cut them up into small pieces. Put them in a wide glass tube, or in a wide-necked bottle such as an empty salad-cream bottle. Press down a wad of tissue paper to keep the laurel in place. Put the beetles into this bottle and cork it tightly. They will become stiff at first but after a while this *rigor mortis* will pass and they will then be ready for setting. A large hard beetle takes longer to relax than a smaller one. If we find that the laurel seems to be losing its power, add a few drops of benzene to the bottle. Some collectors use a chemical called Ethyl Acetate. Only a few drops are needed at a time, and it is best to put them on a piece of blotting paper inside a tube or bottle. Then pop in the beetle and put on the cork at once. With this method the insects do not go stiff at all.

Most beetle collectors set their specimens with the aid of gum on small pieces of stiff card. We can buy a suitable gum from entomological dealers or make our own by mixing three parts of gum tragacanth with one part of gum arabic, moistening it with methylated spirit and then stirring in enough water gradually to make the mixture into the consistency of thin cream. Cut the card into pieces of a suitable size, put a little gum in the centre and then lay the beetle on this, spreading its legs and antennae out carefully on the gummy surface. Leave the card on a setting board to dry, and finally put the specimen away in a store box by fixing a pin through one end of the card. A large beetle will need a pin either end to keep it steady. The correct pins to use for this are called Lill pins. Do not forget to write down the data about the beetle on the back of the card before sticking the insect on. (The word data as used by insect collectors means information about the place where the insect was caught, the date and the name of the person who caught it.)

*   *   *

The Diptera, or two-winged flies, form another huge group of insects, interesting to collect, and to try and identify, but rather difficult, perhaps, for beginners. Even experts find it hard at times to name flies accurately, and often the identification depends on such little things as the number of bristles on the legs. This means that the specimens have to be set very carefully, and with small flies this is a difficult business. Ethyl Acetate, or an ordinary cyanide bottle, is the best thing to use for killing flies.

Pin insects on very small stainless steel pins. They will look neatest if we set their wings out, but this is not strictly necessary. The important thing is to get the legs all visible and spaced out evenly. Use a small setting board and if the legs do not stay put when pulled out insert pins to keep them in place. We need a light and steady hand and good eyesight to set small flies really well, and quite a lot of patience too, so if you feel now that it is too difficult leave flies alone and collect some of the bigger and easier insects instead.

Mosquitoes form quite a small group among the two-winged flies. There are, in fact, only thirty different kinds in Great Britain and we can begin collecting them with a fairly good prospect of being able to form a complete collection. By far the best way of setting about mosquito collecting is to try and find the larvae, which all live in water, and then breed the adults out in captivity. In this way we shall also be able to show empty larval skins and pupae cases, which help to make the collection more interesting.

We find mosquito larvae in stagnant water, and the first place in which to look is the rain-water butt in our own garden. The larvae are small wriggly creatures which come up to the surface to breathe at regular intervals. They are quite easy to capture in a ladle or mug and we can keep them in large jam jars, giving them water from the place where we found them, or at least water which contains plenty of organic matter. Tap water will not do. Ponds, ditches, garden pools, marshes, including salt marshes round the coast, all yield mosquito larvae. There are three species called arboreal mosquitoes which lay their eggs in root holes and hollows between big branches of trees. When it rains these holes fill with water, the eggs hatch and the mosquito larvae complete their life very quickly before the moisture has time to dry up again. Mosquito larvae draw in their air supply through a siphon in their tails, but the pupae, which have large round heads and short curved tails, breathe through two small tubes on the upper side of the body. When the mosquito larvae have changed into pupae it is time to cover the jam jars with fine muslin so that the adult mosquitoes will not escape when they hatch out.

Mosquitoes are usually mounted in rather a different way from ordinary flies. Get some polyporos from a dealer, or, if we can recognize it when it grows as a bracket fungus on birch trees, we can gather some ourselves. Using a sharp razor blade, cut the polyporos into tiny cubes. Push a long pin through each cube to within a quarter of an inch of the head and then insert a second smaller and finer pin at right angles to the first one. Now take out the forceps, grip the smaller pin by the head and after tipping the mosquito out on to a setting board or a sheet of cork, impale it on the tip of this small pin. Try to get the insect in such a position that the pin passes in through one side of the thorax and out through the other, and arrange the wings and legs as well spread out as possible. Write out a small label containing all data and push this on to the larger pin underneath the insect. Then fix the mounted specimen in a store box. The best way to preserve the skins of larvae and pupae is to put them in small tubes in a 50 per cent solution of alcohol.

*   *   *

The study of ants is called Myrmecology, and although ants do not make a very exciting or beautiful collection, they are most interesting insects to observe. There is a great deal to learn about their social system and habits. If we really wish to study ants closely we should try to keep a colony in an observation nest. Many different types of these nests have been invented and dealers can usually supply them, but a very simple way of keeping a small colony of ants is to let them live in a big glass salad bowl, or Pyrex dish.

Put a layer of sand at the bottom of the bowl and then tip into it a colony of ants. Little, newly formed colonies often appear on lawns during the summer, and with a sharp, pointed trowel we can dig one up and dump the whole thing, ants, soil and turf, into the bowl. There will be a great deal of confusion and running around at first, but very soon the ants will calm down and start making a new nest in these unusual surroundings. We can keep the bowl covered with muslin held on by an elastic band, or if the sides are slippery enough there is no need for a cover at all. Alternatively we can stand the bowl on a piece of wood in a tray filled with water so that if any ants stray, they will not be able to start running round the room.

The ants will need moisture at intervals and the best way to give it is simply by watering the bowl with a watering-can fitted with a rose, but do not overdo it so that the whole nest is flooded out. They will also need feeding. We can drop in dead caterpillars and flies, and even give them lumps of sugar at intervals. If we find a leaf or twig covered in greenfly the ants will very much appreciate it and enjoy the honeydew given off by these little insects. We can watch how the ants "milk" the aphids and stroke them with their antennae.

For a collection ants are best killed in a cyanide bottle and it is a good plan to put each insect in a little screw of paper with the data written on it. In this way we can collect a number without getting them muddled. If we have no time to set them at once they can be left in the bottle and will keep in perfect condition for several months. Ants should be set like beetles on little pieces of card, using gum to stick down their bodies, antennae and legs, and any winged individuals should have their wings carefully spread out. When the ants are dry the pieces of card can be pinned in a store box.

*　　　*　　　*

If we camp anywhere near a slow stream or fairly large pond or lake we might be interested in collecting Caddis Flies. The adults are rather similar to moths and usually coloured in grey or brown shades, but if we examine them carefully we shall find that their wings are covered in fine hairs instead of scales. They invariably settle with their wings folded over their bodies in the shape of a steep roof. Their antennae are long and slender and their flight weak. They usually flutter only a short distance before settling to rest. Like moths they are attracted to bright lights at night.

The larvae of the caddis flies are probably better known than the adults; certainly anyone who has ever fished about in ponds for tiddlers and frog spawn is certain to have come across these curious creatures. The great majority of caddis larvae surround their bodies with cases made from grains of sand, pieces of rubbish, bits of water weed leaf, tiny shells, sticks and straws, formed into a tube, which is open at both ends. Inside this tube the grub hides its soft and vulnerable body, while the better protected thorax, head and legs stick out at the front end, but even these can be drawn into the shell when danger threatens.

Most of these case-bearing larvae feed on water weeds and

other vegetable matter at the bottom of ponds and slow streams. But there are other species which do not make this kind of tube at all. They hide away instead under stones, and among dense weeds, and capture living prey in fine silken webs which they spin in front of their hiding-places. These larvae are not so easy to rear in captivity, but the more common tube-dwellers can be kept without any trouble in an ordinary aquarium tank, planted with a good selection of water weeds. If we bring home some caddis worms from a trek we can make an interesting experiment and watch them constructing their tubes.

Do not try to pull any of the worms out of their cases from the front end, because they will almost certainly allow themselves to be pulled to pieces rather than let go with their grappling hooks, but if we insert a match-stick carefully from the other end we can usually push the larvae out without doing them any damage. Remove the old cases from the water, and give the worms some suitable new material such as clean sand, crushed brick, pieces of grass stem, or straw, or even tiny glass beads. We shall then be able to follow the whole process of tube-making from the beginning. Rather than go without "protective clothing" they will make use of anything that is available, even if it is not the kind of material they usually employ.

In Nature each species of caddis worm usually constructs a certain kind of case. It is, therefore, often easier to recognize the different species in the larval stage than as adults and the best way to learn to know them is to keep the larvae singly in jars and see into what kind of caddis flies they eventually turn. When the larvae are full fed they pupate in the water and the adults usually emerge within a few weeks, sometimes after an interval of only four or five days. These should be set in exactly the same way as butterflies and moths. The larvae and pupae are best preserved in small tubes or bottles in spirit or formalin.

*　　　　*　　　　*

Dragon-flies, and the smaller and more delicate damsel-flies, are very beautiful creatures while they are alive, and fairly easy

Some items of equipment for field survey treks. (1) Marching compass, fully calibrated and ideal for cross-country work. (2) Pedometer recording accurately distances walked up to 25 miles. (3) Map measure for tracing a selected route and measuring against a map. (4) Pocket compass. (5) and (6) Map measures for use with maps of all scales. (7) Pocket liquid-filled compass with luminous points. (8) "Dry" compass. (Messrs. Thomas Black & Sons (Greenock) Ltd.).

The Conway Valley, looking north. Rhyd-y-Creuau lies on the east side in the middle distance. The eastern edge of the Carneddau is seen at left, and on the right are the rolling moors of Denbighshire. An ideal countryside for field studies (Howell Evans).

to find and capture, but unfortunately their brilliant colours always fade very soon after they have been killed. A collection of these insects is, therefore, apt to be rather disappointing. It will help a little if we can keep the insects in boxes or breeding cages for a couple of days before killing them, so that the gut has time to empty itself. The best killing medium is Ethyl Acetate. With the bigger dragon-flies it is best to slit the abdomen on the underside after they have been killed, and remove as much of the contents as possible. Then take a small piece of cotton wool, dip it in 70 per cent alcohol, and stuff this into the the cavity to retain the shape of the body. These precautions will prevent the colours from vanishing completely, but a dead dragon-fly is never more than a faded shadow of its once brilliant self and the lustre of the eyes invariably goes. Dragon-flies should be mounted on long pins and their wings set out flat with the front edge of the hind wings at right angles to the body and the long legs spread out. Keep the setting board in as warm a place as possible, as quick drying will help to preserve the colours.

Dragon-fly nymphs can usually be found in all the ponds, pools or slow streams that we are likely to encounter on trek in Britain. If we dredge about in the mud with a net we shall find them. They can be kept in an aquarium tank, but must be fed on live food. When the dragon-flies have emerged we keep the cast skin of the nymph for our collection. During the emerging season we often find these cast skins clinging to the reeds and other plants growing in ponds. The nymphs themselves can be preserved in alcohol.

* * *

Grasshoppers are insects with "an incomplete metamorphosis". This means that they do not go through distinct and separate stages of life such as being first larvae, then resting as pupae, and finally emerging as adults. Instead of this they grow steadily from the time of hatching, go through a series of moults and gradually assume the size and appearance of adults.

Grasshoppers are divided into two distinct groups, the long-

K

horns and the short-horns. The former are distinguished by their very long slender antennae. Some species, such as the Great Green Grasshopper and the Wartbiter, are carnivorous. The short-horns have only stumpy antennae and sometimes the wings never develop. These insects are all vegetarians.

It is quite easy to collect the more common grasshoppers in high summer by sweeping a fairly big net across the grass where they are sitting and chirping. By visiting various types of terrain we can collect quite a number of different kinds. The Great Green Grasshopper, which is a really splendid insect, can be found along the South Coast. In Britain grasshoppers spend the winter in the egg stage, but early in the summer we can collect young insects which are then only miniature replicas of the adults. The vegetable feeders can easily be reared in captivity in a big glass tank, with a cover over it. Keep them well supplied with fresh grass and other green plants.

To kill grasshoppers for a collection we use any of the usual methods. Set the insects on pins, spreading out the wings if these are fully developed, and make sure that the legs and antennae are in natural positions.

Whatever insects, if any, we decide to collect, young people should always bear in mind that there is no point at all in amassing a collection simply in order to be able to boast about the large numbers they have in their store boxes! A field collection is meant to be an aid to field study, and while we collect we can at the same time try to learn as much as possible about the living insects and their habits in the wild state. There are still many gaps in our knowledge of insect behaviour. Amateur entomologists can do a great deal towards helping to fill them.

The Amateur Entomologists' Society is a very useful association. If the reader is interested he should write to the Hon. Advertising Secretary at 18 Golf Close, Stanmore, Middlesex for further information. A postal order for 1s. should be enclosed. For young people under eighteen the annual membership fee is 12s. 6d. The Society issues regular bulletins and also a great number of leaflets dealing with the collecting and preserving of many orders of insects.

Meetings are held where young people can discuss their

hobby with other members who are interested in the same sort
of thing.

FURTHER READING

The Observer's Book of Common British Insects and Spiders—E. F.
     Linssen and L. Hugh Newman (Warne)
Man and Insects—L. Hugh Newman (Aldus Books)
The Pocket Book of British Insects—George E. Hyde (A. & C.
     Black)
The Social Insects—O. W. Richards (Macdonald)
Amateur Entomologists' Society Publications List obtainable
     on receipt of a stamped, addressed foolscap envelope.
     Write to the A.E.S. Publications Agent at 137 Gleneldon
     Road, Streatham, London, S.W.16.

CHAPTER 13

Flowers, Plants and Trees

THE STUDY of wild flowers, trees, grasses and all plants is a fascinating subject, and if one is really keen one can become quite expert. Plant hunting has many advantages over other hobbies and the chief one is that we can pursue it almost everywhere on trek and yet need no costly apparatus. Every camping holiday or hostelling or canoeing holiday we take, and every trek in our own favourite exploring areas, will become much more interesting if we have begun to study the flowers, grasses, trees and ferns which surround us.

The only thing we need is a pocket book dealing with the particular kind of plants we first want to learn about. There are many good books about wild flowers and trees, often in pocket editions, and our bookseller or librarian will help us to choose one that is easy to understand and at the same time fairly comprehensive. Many of these books, especially those which deal with wild flowers, mention only the more usual kinds. There are so many common wild flowers that it will take quite a time to learn their names. Later on, when we begin to look for rarer and more exciting plants, we shall need a more comprehensive guide or a complete flora.

An excellent book for beginners is John Hutchinson's *Common Wild Flowers* (Pelican Books). There are two slim volumes and all the flowers are fully described and illustrated with very clear line drawings. There are also many beautiful photographs and a key to help to identify a plant. *The Concise British Flora in Colour* by W. Keble Martin (Michael Joseph) is excellent for beginners, and it is always possible to borrow special books from a public library or make use of their reference section when we want to identify some particular plant.

We can learn to know and recognize wild flowers without actually becoming a collector and many young people study their hobby in this way. They usually pick one or two specimens of any new plant they find and bring them home to study them carefully. If they happen to find a very rare plant they do not even do this, but simply look at it or perhaps make a sketch or write down a description of it. Personally I think this is the best way of all to study wild flowers. We can be sure then that we do no harm. Many of our rare flowers in Britain are becoming so very scarce that it is a great pity to pick even a single one. In some cases young people who know where these great rarities grow guard the secret carefully, for fear that some thoughtless person might come and uproot the plants.

If someone in the trekking party or youth group can draw and paint a little, or even use coloured crayons intelligently, it helps memory a great deal. Make sketches of *any* interesting plants found. The best way is to have a proper sketch-book, and by the side of each drawing make brief notes of the locality of the flower, the time of year, the size of the plant, its scent (if any), the type of soil and anything else that seems relevant. In this way we gradually build up an album of flower pictures.

At least one member of the youth group may, perhaps, be interested in photography as well as in flowers. In that case two hobbies can be combined with great advantage, compiling a photographic record of all the most interesting plants. Colour photographs would be the ideal thing but most young people find colour photography much too expensive, so we shall have to be content with black and white pictures. A logbook can always note the colour beside each photograph, together with the full data.

On the other hand we may not possess one camera among us, or be able to draw and paint sufficiently well, and may feel that we would rather make a useful collection of plants. There is certainly no harm in this as long as we always remember that rare plants should not be included, however much we may like to have them.

A plant collection is known as a herbarium, and the only satisfactory way of preserving most plants is by pressing and drying them. If we do this carefully we can build up a very fine collection, but the colours of dried plants nearly always fade, and a herbarium can never give a true picture of the beauty of wild flowers.

Don't try to press plants between the pages of books. Why spoil the books as well as the flowers? It is always worth while doing a thing properly and the herbarium is no exception. When we bring home a plant for the collection make sure, first of all, that it is clean and free from grit, slugs or insects. If it is very dirty it will have to be rinsed carefully in water and allowed to dry in the air a little before we try to press it. Choose a suitable place in which to set up the plant press, either on the floor in a corner of a room or on a good strong table. Lay five or six thicknesses of clean smooth newspaper down first of all and then on these a sheet of absorbent paper. We can buy special paper for drying flowers, but firm blotting paper or any non-glossy paper which will absorb moisture will do. Even newspaper will serve if we have nothing else, but sometimes printer's ink stains delicate plants.

Now arrange the plant on the clean paper, spreading it out in as natural a position as possible. Try to get the leaves flat and at least one flower in "full face". This is not easy at first and we may find it best to put on a sheet of covering paper gradually from the bottom, holding the lower parts of the plant in place under this paper while we arrange the flowers and upper leaves.

Sometimes, if the stalk is very thick, or the plant has a solid bunch of leaves at the base, it is best to cut a thin slice away from the back of the stalk with a sharp knife or a razor blade, or remove a few leaves. If we want to show the roots of, say, a dandelion or a wild carrot we must certainly slice it in half, or no amount of pressing will make it flat! Very delicate and fragile plants need to be placed in a folded sheet of thin paper, and then between absorbent paper so that they need not be touched again until they have dried.

When we have managed to arrange the plant to our satisfaction and it is covered with paper, put on some more newspaper and over this a wide board or a piece of thick plywood. A strong square tray is quite a good thing to use and on this we must arrange some weights as evenly as possible. Bricks, or stones, or thick solid books, will all serve, but for the first day or two the weights should not be too heavy. When most of the moisture has dried out of the plants we should increase the weight to get them really flat.

Once the plants are safely in the press we can leave them untouched for a couple of days, but not longer. Remove the weights and the newspaper and take a look at the plants but be careful when the absorbent paper is lifted because the leaves may have stuck to it and we can easily damage the plant at this stage when it is still limp. We shall probably find that the paper is stained from the juice which has been squeezed out from the flowers and leaves, and it may feel quite moist, particularly if we are dealing with a large and succulent plant. In that case we must move the plant carefully on to a clean sheet of paper, otherwise it will not dry out fast enough and may begin to go mouldy. We can hang up the stained paper to dry and use it again another time. With a small and rather dry plant we can often manage by moving it over on to a different part of the paper. Examine the newspaper as well; if that seems damp replace it with dry sheets, and then put the board and the weights back again.

Do not be impatient during this pressing process. It takes quite a time for large plants to become thoroughly dry and well-flattened, and if we take them out too soon they will begin to shrivel. Allow them to remain in the press until they are quite dry and stiff, but not brittle. When this stage is reached they will be ready to mount. For this we should use fairly large sheets of thick stiff paper or thin card. We can fix the flowers on the paper, either by using Seccotine, or gum, applied carefully to the back of the specimen, or by using thin strips of gummed paper stretched across the stalk and the leaves at intervals where it seems necessary. Cut the strips very thin and fix them as neatly as possible. A third alternative is to sew the plant on to the paper with a few stitches across the main stem and the leaf stalks here and there.

Finally we must label each specimen. All the information is written on a sticky label and attached by one edge to the lower left-hand corner of the paper, so that if we have to make any alterations or additions later we can easily tear off the label and replace it by a fresh one. First of all we should put the name of the plant in Latin and English, and if the flower has more than one common name, write them all down. Some old plant names are very quaint. Then fill in the name of the family to which the specimen belongs, the date when it was gathered, the locality and any other information which will help us to remember the plant in the future. Keep the sheets of paper all together in a stiff folder and store the herbarium in a cool dry place. We shall find that it then keeps in good condition for a great many years.

When we have collected and pressed a number of plants we can arrange them in some kind of sequence if the herbarium is to be something more than just a haphazard collection. The most obvious arrangement would be to keep the flowers together in their scientific families such as *Rosaceae*, *Primulaceae*, *Umbelliferae*, etc., putting each group in a labelled folder and placing these in their proper order just as they are set out in the botany books.

Another method is to arrange the plants in natural groups according to the places where they grow. Plant ecology, or the study of plant communities, is a fairly modern and fascinating way of learning about plants and the different soils they prefer. We could begin, for example, by collecting all the plants which we find growing on some typical stretch of heathland, and put them all together in a folder. Then we might choose flowers of the chalk hills and downs, typical meadow flowers, woodland flowers, marsh flowers; each group will give us a comprehensive picture of the vegetation in some particular type of country. If we collect the flowers as they come into bloom right through the flowering season, and then arrange them in order, we shall be able to show the sequence of blooms right through from spring to autumn.

Another good way of starting a plant collection is to make first of all as comprehensive a herbarium as we can of all the

HORNBEAM

BEECH

OAK

SYCAMORE

HORSE CHESTNUT

LIME

ELM

SCOTS PINE

LARCH

ASH

BIRCH

Common British trees which should be known to every camper. Details such as these can be recorded in Field Note-books on trek. The best way to collect leaves is to make leaf prints and arrange them in a photograph album wild plants which we find in a particular terrain, or if we have a fairly large garden, simply those which grow inside our own fence. How many different kinds there are, including the weeds in the kitchen garden! I heard of young people who all joined together and made a collection like this for their parents' silver wedding present. They included both dried and pressed specimens and sketches of every single flower, grass, fern and tree which grew in a four-acre garden. It was a comprehensive record of the plant life on their own domain, and real camping with a purpose, when the purpose is plants!

* * *

Trees

In a collection of herbaceous plants it is often possible to show the whole plant, but if we are going to make a herbarium of trees we must set about it in rather a different way. As far as pressed material is concerned we shall have to be satisfied with showing leaves in various stages of growth and, perhaps, also in their autumn colouring, and the flowers and fruits whenever it is possible to press them. Twigs can be gathered in winter and need only be dried in the air. In the same way we could show samples of bark. But a few twigs and leaves can never give an impression of what a tree really looks like, so if we want to show the habit and general appearance of a tree we must make a small sketch, or take a photograph of a typical tree of each kind, *both in summer and winter*. Deciduous trees look so different when the leaves have fallen. The "skeleton" of a tree is often so very characteristic that we can learn to recognize trees easily even when the branches are quite bare if we make a point of studying their manner of growth and the colour and pattern of their bark. A British school has been very successful in mounting bark rubbings taken on field treks.

The fruits of many trees are attractive things to collect, but often impossible to press, so we must find some other way of preserving them. Ripe bunches of sycamore, hornbeam and ash "keys", and cones of all kinds, will keep perfectly well if they are simply dried in the air. Nuts, acorns and beech mast should first be dried and then painted over with clear varnish to stop

them shrivelling. Many of the firmer berries such as hawthorn
and rowan fruits and rose hips can also be preserved for quite a
time if they are varnished or lacquered. Fruits like this can
either be stored in drawers or boxes, or if we have an eye for
artistic arrangement we could group them together in a show-
case, fixing them with fine wire or strong carpenter's glue.
Show-cases like this are often used for butterflies and can
be bought from natural history dealers. A shallow drawer
from some old cabinet will make an excellent show-case if we
fit a piece of glass over the front to keep out the dust. It might
record the results of one camping or hostelling trek for years.

★   ★   ★

Grasses

Grasses are far more difficult to identify than ordinary flowering plants. We may very well feel discouraged at not being able
to name them correctly without a great deal of trouble. A book
with really good illustrations is a help, but there is no reason
why we should not make a collection of grasses even if we
cannot name them all. A single meadow in which we pitch our
tents can furnish us with an amazing number of different kinds.
In one way I think grasses are perhaps the most satisfactory of
all plants for a collection; they are very easy to press, and even
when dry and flat they still look far more natural than most
other plants. Mount them on sheets of paper exactly as for
flowering plants, and then arrange them according to locality,
or in their botanical order.

We may, perhaps, be more interested in the beauty of grasses
than in their botanical characteristics, and feel that we should
like to display them in a more attractive way than singly on
separate sheets in a herbarium. In that case one suggestion is to
make a grass picture, using as many different kinds as we can
find. We can gather the heads either when they are actually in
flower early in June, or a little later, when the seeds are beginning to plump up. Then dry them and press them in the usual
way. When we have collected enough arrange them as attrac-
tively as possible on a fairly large sheet of white or tinted card.
Fix each grass straw down with dabs of modellers' balsa

cement on the back and hide the ends of the stalks under a few pressed leaves or a fern frond. When the picture is complete cover it with a sheet of glass or cellophane, and hang it on the wall. Girls are especially good at this kind of "end to a perfect trek" picture.

*   *   *

Mosses, Lichens, Ferns and Fungi

All the mosses and a great many lichens are quite easy to dry and press and as they are comparatively small we can mount several different kinds on the same sheet of paper. Do not gather lichens when they are very dry, because many of them are then so brittle that they break to pieces at the slightest touch. In a damp condition they bear handling much better.

Ferns are delightfully easy to press and the fronds, by nature already more or less flat, retain a natural appearance even in the herbarium. When we mount our specimens we should show also the underside of a leaf, with the brown spore pustules which are arranged in different ways in the various species. We can collect spore patterns alone by suspending fern leaves a couple of inches above sheets of paper coated with gum and leaving them for a few days in a perfectly still atmosphere. The spores will fall down on to the paper and stick to the gummed surface.

Fungi are very interesting things to study but not so easy to collect. They are an enormous family, which include a great many plant diseases such as rots, rusts and moulds, but these are too difficult for anyone but a real expert. If we keep only to the larger fungi, such as mushrooms and toadstools and the various species that grow on the stems of both dead and living trees, we shall have more than enough material for a collection. Most of the fungi appear in the autumn and winter when there are very few flowering plants to be seen, so this is a hobby that can be carried on, as it were, in the "off season". Fungi can be a first-class reason for autumn and winter hikes using youth hostels, or farms.

Some of the more woody kinds of fungi can be preserved

simply by drying in the air and will keep like this for years. Others which are small and not too fleshy can be pressed just like ordinary plants. The fairy-ring fungus, for example, and small specimens of the chanterelle, will press satisfactorily if we gather them in dry weather and change the absorbent paper frequently. Larger and more solid fungi like the various forms of Boletus, the parasol mushroom and the Fly Agaric are almost impossible to press but we can preserve them in a 10 per cent solution of formalin, or in strong brine, in closed jars or bottles, but they will lose their colour in time. The best method of making a record of fungi is really to sketch them or take photographs. We can also collect spore patterns in the same way as with ferns. The easiest way is to make a hole in the centre of a piece of gummed card, slip the stem of the fungus through this and push the card up so that it is just below the under surface of the fungus, but not actually touching it. If the fungus is ripe the spores will immediately begin to fall on to the paper.

*   *   *

Seaweeds

Seaweeds are also plants. If we spend our summer camps regularly by the seaside we could easily make quite a comprehensive collection. The great difficulty with many of the finer and more delicate kinds of seaweed, which are also the most beautiful, is to get them on to paper in anything like their natural positions, because as soon as they are removed from the water they collapse and cling together in a tangled mass.

There is, however, a way of overcoming this problem. When we bring a piece of seaweed home, we must put it at once in a basin of fresh water and wash it very thoroughly to get rid of salt and sand. We may have to change the water several times. Have some stiff mounting paper ready, and when the piece of seaweed is floating in perfectly clean water, slide the paper carefully under it and lift it up, on the paper, allowing the water to run off gently to one side. In this way we should get the weed in a natural spreading position, although we may have to adjust a frond here and there with a fine paintbrush. Lay the sheet down on a table and allow the weed to dry naturally in the room until we can no longer notice any surface moisture. Then cover it with absorbent paper and begin the pressing very gradually, with only light weights for the first few days and frequent changes of paper.

Just like grasses, the fine green and red seaweeds can be mounted under glass, making colourful pictures. In Victorian times such seaweed bouquets were very fashionable but we hardly ever see them now and the few that remain have long since faded and lost their beauty. If campers have the courage to revive an old idea a seaweed picture is a very good way of displaying a collection for a few years.

Books of special interest for seaside projects are *The Seaside Nature Book* by E. F. Daglish (Dent) and *The Seaside Pocket Companion* by Hugh Stoker (Hutchinson).

FURTHER READING

Common Wild Flowers—John Hutchinson (Pelican; 2 vols.)

The Concise British Flora in Colour—W. Keble Martin (Michael Joseph)

Wild Flowers—John Gilmour (Collins)

Wild Flowers of Chalk and Limestone—J. L. Lousley (Collins)

Wayside and Woodland Blossoms—Edward Step (revision by A. B. Jackson and A. Keith Jackson), (Warne; 3 vols.)

Wayside and Woodland Trees—Edward Step (revision by A. B. Jackson and A. Keith Jackson), (Warne)

Wayside and Woodland Ferns—Edward Step (revision by A. B. Jackson), (Warne)

The Observer's Book of British Ferns—W. J. Stokoe (Warne)

The Forester's Handbook—H. L. Edlin (Thames and Hudson)

Collins Guide to Mushrooms and Toadstools—Morten Lange and F. B. Hora

CHAPTER 14

Outdoor Collecting Hobbies

WE ALL collect something at some stage or other in our lives, from stamps and cheese labels to fine old silver, pewter, china or ships in bottles. The collecting may be done in fits and starts, or may begin in our youth and grow into a lifelong interest, absorbing most of our free time.

Young people are invariably enthusiastic collectors, and this can be turned to good account as far as outdoor field work is concerned. It makes a fine introduction to serious field work in geology, for instance, to trek along stony upland streams making a collection of water-worn pebbles of outstanding beauty and colour. Such a collection can easily be displayed in a cabinet with a six-inch map mounted alongside, showing the trekking route and where particular pebbles were found. If photos are taken and added to the mounted map so much the better.

In the same way we can collect sand and soil samples in a wide variety of terrain, displaying them neatly in small glass-topped boxes with all relevant data added on the side in Indian ink, or even cardboard "pill-boxes" with "Perspex" lids are just as effective. My experience is that lightweight camping and youth hostelling treks are especially suitable as a means to an end in such work, and that teenage boys and girls react well to simple collecting treks. In fact the enthusiasm may need to be curbed if we are to get on with other field work, and thus keep specimen collecting in its right perspective. I might add one vital piece of practical advice at this stage. On all such treks keep the actual specimens *tightly* contained in stout sealed envelopes or muslin bags with all relevant data noted at once in the daily field book. Furthermore, carry all such specimens for the rest of the trek in a rucksack kept for the purpose. There is nothing more disappointing or disheartening for young people than to arrive at an overnight camp site or hostel and find that precious specimens of sands and soils are hopelessly mixed up, or have somehow found their way into sleeping-bags, or even the butter.

*   *   *

I have sifted many trek reports and field books to find "collecting treks" which brought much fun and enjoyment to parties of young people. Before I go into these in more detail let us briefly think about the approach.

In general we try to "collect" something or other which does not have to be carried, though if we are keen on geology then we can collect pebbles and rocks and soils and sands. But all such specimens have to be carried, or possibly posted home. Geological treks are rather a special case, and more suitable for older boys and girls with a good deal of outdoor experience.

In general we shall try and collect things which will not add to packed kits and thereby cause fatigue and a lowering of morale and enthusiasm towards the end of a hot day in late spring or summer. Adolescents may often overtire themselves on trek without being aware of it, and the adult leader must watch for such signs of strain and act accordingly. I have always found it best to temper enthusiasm with common sense and caution when necessary, but without ever losing the spark of adventure. It is better to finish the day's trek and field work knowing that the party could have gone on for another hour than to find next morning that the previous day's toil was too exacting and nothing can be started, if at all, until the afternoon. Leaders soon find these practical considerations out for themselves. There is an art in selecting the right people for trekking, and making up teams of the same age groups and standards of achievement. If there is a doubt about someone, be ruthless (in a very kindly way) and leave the doubtful one out. What matters most of all is the efficiency and spirit and harmony of the team as a whole in the field.

Page 17: CHILTERNS TREK
Day 4: 16th JULY 1953

TIME	MILES	PLACE	NOTES & ROUTE
1050	41	Seymour Green	
1123	42	Cookley Green	undulating pleasant green hills photos. saw mitt 32/34 stile
1148	44	Park Corner	OXFORD ← Avoid main road Henley-Oxford traffic heavy ← Goldfinches
1235	45½	Nettlebed (Camp-site)	Check on Grim's Ditch Campsite Smiley's Farm ?
LUNCH			Sketch church, 2 stiles, Joyce Errington
1515	48	Highmoor Cross	Good walking Ridgeway lanes to Leck
			Settle site for night Stay Hotel (invited Television!)
			Map O.S. 159 One Inch Site charge 2/- tent Lunch Nettlebed say 3/6

Dull but Dry
Reputed Battery at Assendon
Sunny
sketch 23 Old Kiln
Joyce Errington
Beech Woods (chalk)
Squirrel hunts in progress
HENLEY
READING

The author recommends that treks should be recorded in loose-leaf note-books of this simple pattern. Artists' sketch-books and waterproof pencils may be used. All relevant information is recorded in clear, concise fashion; photographs and sketches may be added.

*A plane tabler at work in the field, making a map by conventional ground
survey methods (the Ordnance Survey).*

We collect effortlessly, then, using cameras and ciné-cameras, note-books, or sketch-books if we are artists, and ensuring that every place where we stop to use a camera or sketch is identified and pin-pointed on the maps we are carrying. In general the one-inch O.S. map will be sufficient, the pin-pointed position being ringed with a small circle in Indian ink, and numbered or lettered. For the best work six-inch maps are advised because we can put so much field information directly on to the maps, and then when we get back home, or return to base camp, the maps can be mounted and clear varnished, giving a permanent record of the trek. Such mapboards can then be hung up in classroom, Scout Group, Guide company or youth club headquarters. They will be of value in later work with other parties, or important as an inspiration to others to go and do likewise— and in their own way if they do not care for that particular method.

*　　　*　　　*

Camera work can be improved by reading clearly-written, sensible books on the subject and seeking all the practical assistance possibly from a good photographer. I particularly recommend the work of Dr. G. L. Wakefield, of the Faculty of Technology at Manchester University. He has long experience of teaching the art of photography to young people in a practical and interesting way.

Outdoor tips for good photography include the following practical advice for emphasis to young people:

1. Keep the lens and camera especially clean. There is a great deal more dirt about on a camping trek than we may realize. Cameras need extra protection in tents particularly.
2. Observe all the accepted rules of good photography and don't waste valuable film when miles from the nearest chemist or source of replenishment.
3. Country folk in everyday clothes and surroundings are always good subjects for beginners—in fact, start with a collection of country characters. We need not worry about movement in such photos.

L

4. Old buildings and landscapes are safe and solid subjects. They always stand perfectly still! They give adequate proof, too, as to whether we can stand still and take "straight" pictures. Remember to put a friend in a building picture to give an idea of relative size, and also in a landscape picture to give some idea of perspective.

5. To take photos inside a famous old house or building look for rooms with plenty of windows and light. Try and put the camera on a seat or table, using a time exposure.

6. In camp we try to get happy, everyday pictures, and the ones our party will want to keep are invariably natural and "action" pictures. Keep to the rules and take pictures under the best natural conditions.

*   *   *

Ideas for "collecting" treks can be suited to the tastes and capabilities of the group concerned. If we are crossing "green" country and trekking along, say, Offa's Dyke (or part of it) along the border of England and Wales, or elsewhere in North Wales, we find ourselves constantly climbing stiles. Farmers have been using stiles as a means of access to their land since medieval times, and have still to find a better method of keeping their livestock in bounds while allowing a right of way to the public. There are many quaint examples of stiles, and a competent photographer or an amateur artist can make up a really interesting logbook. (The idea would be to use the same size of loose-leaf field book all the time, so that eventually all sketches done by the party can be collated and kept in one loose-leaf logbook.)

Reece Winstone, a well-known professional photographer, has a vast collection of photographs of stiles: they show there is real "style in stiles". The variety of British stiles is so remarkable that in one "stile trek" alone (using Youth Hostels) one party of young people made a collection with camera and sketch-book of almost fifty examples. Another trek in 1968 yielded eighty-six.

Milestones give plenty of scope to collectors on trek. They

were removed when invasion threatened Britain in 1940 but were restored in the great majority of cases after 1945. They have outlived their original purpose in our age of speed, but are part of the British heritage and well worth recording: eighteenth- and nineteenth-century milestones are especially worth hunting out. An original and amusing collection of scarecrows has also been made on trek. The specimens were photographed and sketched.

*   *   *

Fences are of special interest to all outdoor lovers, no matter what their age might be. Farms, and the hedges separating fields around them, are often of great age. We can learn much about them on our very camp sites, and about farming methods and local traditions at the same time.

When Britain was farmed on the strip system fences were quite unknown. The strips were indicated by boundary stones, with occasional rough or temporary fences to keep animals out of growing wheat, oats or barley, but this kind of farming was an impracticable business. Cattle and horses had to be fed in winter, and farmers needed good clover, hay, and root crops for the purpose. So fences came into being.

Early treks in the hills (for instance, in the West Country, and particularly Devon) can follow old fences creeping along the contours and ending obviously where the gradient became too steep for the plough. Thick fences made of turf and rock are also to be found in hilly districts. They were erected to prevent good fertile top soil being washed away into the valleys and river bottoms.

If a trekking party takes soil samples on either side of a hedge fence in hilly country they are sometimes found to be quite different. Old hedges were often planted, in fact, to mark the division between good soil and indifferent soil, or clay. That idea saved time, labour and seed in the planting season. Natural features of the water system, such as ditches and feeders of streams, were also natural boundaries of fences. In North and Central Wales, and in the Yorkshire Dales, and the Border country, old fences often sprawl up steep hill-sides for no apparent reason. Such fences once divided the grazing areas of sheep, when wool was just as important then as coal is to us today. I once did a plane table survey of old fences of this character in North and Central Wales, using my own light-weight camping equipment. I can truly say it was the most rewarding trek imaginable, if strenuous.

"Fence spotters" can find out for themselves some of the great variations in boundary hedges. Within the boundaries of his own farm a farmer never erected formidable fences or hedges. But neighbours often faced thorn! Elsewhere hedges were planted for special utility purposes. Ash is a fine, hard wood much in demand for the handles of spades, ploughs and farm tools; so an ash hedge is sure to be around an old farm some-where. Sheep farmers needed hurdles, especially at lambing-time in an exposed situation to keep out cold ground winds, or to keep the sheep together at certain times of the year. Hazel hedges supplied the raw material for the hurdles.

If we identify an unusual shrub or tree in a hedge when on trek we can also try to hazard the reason for its planting. There are countless cases of windbreak hedges, too, planted to protect young stock in the farm-yards as well as the farmer's wife going about her lawful duties. Mapping the position of walnut trees in hedges has been a favourite project in Southern schools.

Sometimes climatic factors were of great importance in the erection of fences and hedges, and in other cases there may be historical reasons. Ralph Wightman, for instance, is not certain why there are so many double hedges in West Dorset, with room for narrow footpaths between them. There might have been some doubt about the growth of such hedges. Possibly the second outer hedge was some form of protection, or safe-guard, so that gaps could be replaced quickly and easily. There may be a number of solutions.

There is a climatic reason for the relatively low lanes of Western Anglesey which are often below the general level of the surrounding fields, with high earth banks to heighten the effect. This is a form of protection against a powerful prevailing westerly wind. We can trek along those lanes on a windy day and scarcely be conscious of the breeze. Devon has its high earth-banked lanes in very similar fashion. They also may have some climatic explanation. But lanes below the general level of surrounding fields are often old trackways of great age.

Once young people start "collecting" fences and hedges in this way we may find it difficult to know when to stop. Eventually we can restrict ourselves to "collecting" types that we have never seen before, thus building up a unique "fence and hedge log".

*   *   *

Old bridges, ancient monuments (such as cromlechs), trade signs, church bells, horse brasses, ancient churches, church brasses, old fire marks (the early fire-brigade signs), forges, village crafts and customs, noble trees, unique country cottages, tithe barns, toll bars, turnpikes, odd railway bridges, and even the collecting of specimens of seaweeds have all been "collected" by young people.

An entertaining search can be made for "old-time punishments". One trekking party set out to discover ancient stocks, ducking stools, miscreant cells, whipping posts, pillories and so on. Once found they were photographed or sketched. Spotting varieties of village pumps was another good idea.

Horse brasses are good fun as a long-term idea to the individual genuine collector who is interested only in real brasses and not the commercial modern ones made in Birmingham. Genuine brasses are not easy to find, but they invariably have marks where the shanks were removed clearly visible on the reverse. I have picked up a number of genuine ones in villages in out-of-the-way places on the map, including a rare Christian cross and some of the New Forest pony brasses. The genuine miniature horse brass can sometimes be found at country horse shows and fairs, and sometimes in an out-of-the-way forge. I say "long term" as far as horse brasses are concerned because in many years of trekking I have only managed to find about thirty genuine brasses and six miniatures. But it is good fun looking for them!

Old bridges are always worth recording. Canoeists can find as much pleasure here as campers and hostellers, noting the types and kinds of bridge under which they pass. G. Bernard Wood, official photographer to the National Buildings Record, was a great collector of bridges—by camera, of course. He always found out everything possible about the bridge he photographed, such as the name of the person who built it and the kind of tracks linked with it (packhorse route, turnpike road and so on). The structure itself may be of unusual interest. There may be a sundial on the parapet, or an imposing gateway or arch at one end, or there might even be a chapel or building perched on it.

Early specimens "collected" by Mr. Wood included the rough slabs of stone stretching over streams known as monolith or clapper bridges. They can be found on Dartmoor, Exmoor, Malham (Yorkshire) and Wycollar (Lancashire). Together with rough-hewn tree-trunks they were the earliest of all bridges.

Druid's Bridge, at Wycollar, is a perfect specimen of this type of bridge, but downstream there is a bridge of three stone slabs supported in the middle by stone pillars in the stream bed. This "Weaver's Bridge" was made by surmounting the stepping-stones with a footway that could be used in times of flood. At Wycollar, once noisy with the clumping of clogged cotton weavers, there is also a fine packhorse bridge with a double archway but tiny parapets only a few inches high that need some explanation. In the early nineteenth century such parapets allowed ample clearance for the bulging panniers of "jagger" ponies, as they were called, carrying goods all over the North Country. Not far away, in Oxenhope, a packhorse bridge has three steps cut at either end for the purpose of lifting panniers clear of bridge parapets.

Our ancestors thought nothing of building on a bridge. (Examples worth following up are at High Bridge, Lincoln; Wakefield; Rotherham; and St. Ives, Huntingdonshire.) There are "fortified bridges", as at Monmouth, where young people can find something dear to their hearts—apertures through which boiling oil was poured to add novelty to the battle raging below.

There are medieval bridges of odd shape, like the zigzag

bridge across the Little Ouse at Brandon. There are hundreds of bridges with stories of their own such as Beggar's Bridge at Glaisdale, near Whitby. A beggar, Tom Ferres, was so tired of swimming across the River Esk at this point that he swore to build a bridge there when he became rich. He did so, and after 300 years it still stands.

There is a sundial on the parapet of the old Brider Bridge at Berwick-on-Tweed, and other bridges with remarkable inscriptions on them. Linnel's Bridge, near Hexham, is one fine example, and there can be a place in the field-book for a note of any mason's marks or symbols which we may find on such a bridge.

*   *   *

There is not space to deal with church brass-rubbings in detail here, but it is no longer as easy to take rubbings (with pencil or heelball on thick tracing paper) as it used to be. Many country clergymen rightly object to indiscriminate rubbings being taken without permission, for it is all too easy to damage a valuable or unique brass. The adult in charge of a trekking party wanting to do such work should *always* seek the advice and help of local clergy, and give a donation to the funds of the church for taking a rubbing. In some country churches the clergy charge a fee, usually in the region of 1s. to 10s. for taking brass rubbings and also stipulate that they must be done under their own supervision. This has the effect of discouraging novices, and also ensures that damage is not done to ancient churches.

A most useful book for those who are interested on finding out more about old churches is *How to Explore Churches* by Kenneth A. Lindley, published by the Educational Supply Association. It has good illustrations and useful lists of "Things to Find Out" and "Things to Do", and has been used with great success in school work.

FURTHER READING

Photographic books, including titles written by Dr. G. L. Wakefield; see Focal Press and Fountain Press lists.

The County History section of the local public library, together with any publications of the County Archaeological Societies. A local librarian will undoubtedly be able to suggest a reading list for the area chosen.

CHAPTER 15

Archaeology and Geology

GEOLOGY

GEOLOGY may seem a dull subject at first glance, but it can be a first-class reason for undertaking a lightweight camping or youth hostelling trek. A leader with a spark of enthusiasm for the fascinating study of rocks and land forms can soon persuade a party of young people to see what fun it is and can be. Moreover, we can pitch tents in a suitable area and hammer away at a cliff face for hours in the search for fossils and do no damage at all! But careless or haphazard digging by amateurs can ruin an archaeological "dig", and extreme care must be taken.

Some excellent School Journey Parties with geological aims have been undertaken with the utmost help and co-operation of the Youth Hostels Association. Some kind of preliminary hostelling trek or cycle-tour reconnaissance of a selected area or areas is necessary if young people are to get the "feel" of geology. It is useless to set out with enthusiasm on a hunt for fossils if we have no idea of what geology is all about. Early treks, lightweight camps and cycle tours can all be designed to give a broad appreciation of geology and its importance is determining the face and physical character of Britain.

The Shropshire-Welsh Border is ideal walking country. If we plan an hostelling expedition we can stay at the hostels at Shrewsbury, Wilderhope Manor and Ludlow. Then a trek can be planned to find where the hills of Wales meet the broad plains of the Midlands. One party, in the Stiperstones, Lawley, Caradoc, Long Mynd and Wrekin area, discovered where

ancient outliers of Cambrian rocks projected, as it were, the
hilly nature of Wales on to the gentle, undulating contours of
the Midlands beyond the Silurian limestone of Wenlock Edge.
It would not need much additional study of the Ordnance
Survey, and the geological, maps of the area to discover more
equally exciting treks on the Welsh Border.

Sometimes people get the feeling that the only worthwhile
exploring country in Britain is in the Lake District, Devon and
Cornwall, North Wales and the Highlands of Scotland, because
these areas are the best known and most talked about. How
wrong they are! Of course these areas *are* first-class. Gentle
"green country" does mean a lack of exciting contours. But it
does not mean dullness, or a lack of variety in the type of terrain. It is important to impress on young people that they are
likely to find adventure anywhere in Britain for the seeking. If
an area *seems* "dull" it is because we are dull ourselves, not the
terrain. We should not always require the stimuli of rock faces,
screes, or a buzzard on some gaunt fell, as spurs to activity and
achievement.

School Journey Parties, for instance, can find much useful
geological work to do in the Eastern Counties, which are on
the drier side of Britain, let me remind youth leaders, and usually
mean longer trekking time outdoors in summer. One party has
studied, in mid-week, when hostel life is quiet, the chalk out-
crop and the Cromer moraine and seen the contrast with low-
lying fens and the area of the Broads. A youth leader who is also
a geographer would know at once that it is a classic area for
studying glaciation in Britain, as well as subsidence and the
changing courses of rivers. There are many areas in Britain
where geology can be combined with hostelling in this way.
(Botanists are well provided with hostels in the Fen country,
and the 400 square miles of heathland around Thetford known
as "Breckland" is a paradise for them.)

*   *   *

I would suggest a cycle tour of Anglesey as another useful
preliminary to geological study, partly because it is a compact
island at relatively low levels especially suitable for young

people awheel, and also because it is a geological gem, with so much to see and do in a small confine. Let us look at Anglesey a little more closely.

The island is gently undulating, yet never dull. If we lengthen the trek to include the nearby rocky Lleyn Peninsula we have a tour of rare contrast and beauty. It lies within easy reach of the great industrial areas of South Lancashire, South Yorkshire and the Midlands. Parties who live in Manchester, Liverpool, Birmingham, Leeds, Nottingham or Sheffield can go to North Wales by train with bicycles in the guard's van. The tour can then start at some convenient point such as Bangor and, indeed, I would recommend this to avoid the long and tiring ride along the North Wales coast.

There are superb beaches and many secluded, rocky coves in Anglesey, plus the added attraction of Snowdonia, purple and magnificent, constantly before us. The best way to tour Anglesey by cycle is to go right round the coast, keeping as near the shore line as possible and completely avoiding the A.5 road that crosses the island from Bangor to Holyhead. The map to use is the O.S. 1 inch to 1 mile, Popular Edition No. 41. It does not much matter which way we go, but I suggest an anti-clockwise route once across Menai Bridge. The route will then be Beaumaris–Penmon–Red Wharf Bay–Benllech–Amlwch and Bull Bay–Cemaes Bay–Llanfaethlu–Valley –Four Mile Bridge–Holy Island–Rhoscolyn–return to Valley via Trearddur Bay, South Stack and Holyhead—then Caergeiliog–Rhosneigr–Aberffraw–Malltraeth–Newborough—then return to Menai Bridge, and continue touring in the Lleyn Peninsula as far as Aberdaron and Bardsey Island if there is time.

So much for the route. For a small party Gilwell Hike tents will provide excellent accommodation. Take local advice when pitching camp for the night, for in Anglesey the prevailing westerly breeze can be very strong, even in summer. It is always best to site the tent in the lee of a bank, tall hedge, haystack or barn, or it may show an alarming tendency to "take off". On the west coast a morning mist blows in from the sea in summer but invariably disappears by mid-morning.

Do not let it deceive the party into thinking bad weather has set in for the day.

The road and lane surfaces are good and we need little more than ordinary touring kit. If the weather is very hot and dry, protection for the eyes is needed around Newborough warren and sand-dunes. Take camera, note-book and pencil, sketching block, swim trunks (magnificent swimming is available in all parts, but swim only where local people say it is safe). The people of Anglesey are warm-hearted and generous and will help youth groups to enjoy their touring holiday if asked for their advice and help. Especially remember not to leave field gates open; or walk or cycle across growing crops even if it does "look like grass"; or to disturb farm dogs or grazing cattle.

Plan this tour with the help of the one-inch map and try to understand this fascinating county of contrast. Make as many notes as possible. See if there is a reason for some of the odd things jotted down. A field of growing oats may be very patchy in texture if rock is close to the surface. A "mantle of drift soils", as the geographer calls it, is responsible for the fertility of the island. Note stretches of almost barren rock on the western side, with gorse and heather-covered commons. That irregular coast would be even more pronounced if the island were stripped of these drift soils. Note how the marked headlands of Holyhead mountain or Point Lynas descend sheer into the sea. At Trearddur Bay see how the silting of an old tidal strait has joined what were once two separate parts of the island. This contrasts strongly with the long sandy bays of Rhosneigr but a mile or two to the south. Everywhere signs of encroachment can be seen. Old roads and tracks end apparently at the water's edge, but reappear again on the other side of the inlet. Some coastal roads on the western part of the isle may only be used with safety at low tide.

The original church of St. Fraed at Trearddur, founded in the fifth century, has long since disappeared, and a hundred yards of land in Rhosneigr were worn away in fifty years. Small lakes, such as Lake Maelog, have been formed by blown sand blocking up a former arm of the sea. On the north coast at Cemlyn Bay there is a tidal lagoon made by a shingle ridge raised twenty feet during a single storm in 1859. Wave erosion in the past has worn back the heads of bays so rapidly that at Red Wharf Bay the low cliffs of drift may be a mile or so further inland than at the beginning of historic times. The resistant headlands stand out everywhere sharply.

The tremendous wave attack of the sea on the coast of Anglesey is most impressive. Note how at certain points, particularly on Holy Island, and near Trwyn Bychan on the north coast, the sea is in a state of advance against solid rock but has been helped considerably by landslips.

Much of Anglesey is low-lying and below fifty feet even. If a little while is spent studying the 100-foot contour line on the map it will be seen that another subsidence of 100 feet would result in most of the county becoming flooded. Only a small subsidence would be necessary to make another Menai Straits parallel to the present one along the line of the Cefni and Afon Ceint streams. Look at it when arriving at Malltraeth.

The woods on the island include private plantations and copses. The only real natural woodland is on the sheltered eastern side of the island. The remaining woodlands are poor and stunted in growth and are gradually being killed by climbing ivy. In all cases the effect of strong westerly winds can be seen in the woods, the trees being remarkably bent over as a direct result. There are plenty of instances of this. The absence of trees is in fact a characteristic feature of the Anglesey landscape, but this is the result of Man's folly. At one time Anglesey was a well-wooded island with plenty of groves for the Druids.

*   *   *

There is no need to make geology treks difficult. Much of my own field work in geography, geology and archaeology has been done with groups of young people from secondary and grammar schools, or with students at training colleges and universities. All we need do in the early stages is to emphasize land forms and particularly the processes of weathering of rocks, both natural and chemical, and the action of such natural agents as frost, heat, wind, running water, ice and the atmosphere. There are enough suggestions here for geological treks galore, and much depends on where a youth group lives. We can enlist the help of the geography master at the nearest grammar school to ascertain what is possible within, say, a twenty-mile area of our particular town or suburb. Or if we live in a city with a university there will no doubt be a department of geography, and possibly a department of geology, too. In several cases, to my knowledge, a lecturer or reader on the staff of such a department was able to give useful field tasks to parties of senior grammar-school boys and girls going on trek. Geology is primarily an open-air subject, and the work which has to be done in laboratories is always based on solid, sound field work. There is scope for collections of rock, sand and soil specimens, fossils and so on, and all this work can be done initially in a room at the youth hostel (the warden may be able to arrange the use of a room).

*   *   *

In the following list I have collated the work and experience of a number of geological treks by young people using tents or youth hostels, in the belief that they will be of value to others contemplating such work. In some cases they were school or college journey parties in charge of a responsible adult who was either a master or lecturer in geography or an allied subject. In other cases they were small parties of older Scouts, or members of a youth club, in charge of an amateur geologist. (In one case this adult happened to be employed by an oil company in a geological capacity.)

1. A study of river drainage on the moors of North Yorkshire, and especially of river capture by the River Derwent near Malton.
2. A study of glaciation in the Lake District.
3. A study of glaciation in Snowdonia.
4. A trek following the River Severn from mouth to source, with special emphasis on geological features.
5. A study of river meanders on the River Wharfe near Kettlewell: in this particular instance a standing camp of lightweight tents was set up for seven days.

6. Studies of erosion by the sea at a variety of points on the coast wherever we may live in Britain. This is a task which is fairly easy to plan and carry through. Suitable points might be the Lancashire coastline, East Anglia (around Cromer), East Yorkshire (around Flamborough Head), and Durham (between the Tyne and the Wear).

7. A study of fault scarps in the Pennines, and especially Giggleswick Scar and Attermire Scar.

8. A particularly good geological study is the Great Whin Sill of Northumberland and Durham. Sills are fascinating because they often extend such a long way, where the magma or volcanic material that has been forced upwards and outwards has found its way between the bedding planes of a well-bedded rock and so spread out. If the sheet has a consistent thickness but is fairly thin, at any rate geologically speaking, we call it a sill. In the Great Whin Sill—Britain's largest—dolerite has intruded into carboniferous limestone. We can follow it from the cliffs along the coast south of Bamborough Castle to more inland cliffs across the south of Northumberland. The famous Roman Wall is built on the very crest of these cliffs and therefore we can do a "double-purpose" trek in the area, looking at the geology and at the Roman Wall. One reason for the Wall's remarkable survival is the geological fact that a sill is harder than the sedimentary rocks into which it was intruded, and therefore it has resisted weathering. We need not bother young people with more technical terms than are necessary, but if they are willing to spend an hour discussing the geology of sills they will appreciate the Roman Wall trek all the more.

9. Rainfall and water supply are always worth studying. The Y.H.A. produce a film strip on School Journey Parties which shows how a trek was organized by a Birmingham girl's school to a reservoir and dam in Central Wales to study Birmingham's water supply. This has already been dealt with in more detail in Chapter 2.

Geology is a practical outdoor study and the amateur geologist needs a practical kit. Since it is a reasonable load, geologists may well prefer to use youth hostels rather than tents, but kit can always be sent on by post if camping has to be undertaken in an area where no hostels exist.

A geological hammer is square in section with a square face at one end and a chisel edge at the other, made at right angles to the shaft. It is 2 lb. to 3 lb. in weight, while a "trimmer" or light hammer ($\frac{1}{2}$ lb.) is used to trim material obtained with the heavier hammer. In addition to these hammers the following equipment is needed: chisel(s); linen bags for collecting samples; plenty of spare sugar packets for the same purpose; haversacks for carrying kit and samples; a compass for determining the directions of structure and dip of rock strata; a clinometer (a simple instrument for measuring the degree of slope) which we use for noting the actual dip of the strata.

The usual field note-books and maps are carried, but simple geological symbols need to be known, and I cannot do better than recommend readers to read and act on Chapter Sixteen of Dr. A. Raistrick's excellent book, *Teach Yourself Geology*, which can act as a guide to any field party.

Lastly, I would urge youth leaders not to make heavy weather of a geological trek. Find an initial way of interesting young people in it, as we did with a cycle tour of Anglesey, and from some simple beginning like that build up to a trek in earnest along the Pennine Way or the Roman Wall. It may be more suitable for seniors of stamina and good physique but it is well worth it. If we carry hammers and go hunting for strata and fossils remember that "stone bashing" can be *very* tiring!

ARCHAEOLOGY

Archaeology, says Dr. Ian Cornwall of the Institute of Archaeology, London, is "the science which studies human culture through its material equipment". But other sciences have important contributions to make towards its fulfilment, and in this sense geology is "a handmaid of prehistory". I feel it is important for young people to know something about geology in the field before they rush into archaeology, which can be truly fascinating. An excavation, or "dig" as we call it in more homely fashion, attracts everyone, and since tremendous damage can be done by enthusiastic but novice teenagers on such digs let it be said at once that experienced adult supervision is always necessary.

Individual senior boys, particularly if they are camping within call, can be extremely useful on summer "digs", carting barrow-loads of soil about and helping to hoist pans of earth and rocks and so on from trenches. They will learn a great deal in the process, and in time may wish to join their own local archaeo-logical societies and thus take a wider interest in prehistory.

*   *   *

I showed earlier in this chapter how a cycle tour of Anglesey was used to stimulate an interest in geology among several groups of young people from the Midlands. The same route was also used at a later date to infuse a background of archaeo-logy into the same youth groups.

This is how it was tackled in a very practical approach:

The island is rich in prehistoric remains and the majority of them have been well preserved, but great difficulty has been experienced in dating some of them. The very fact that Angle-sey was an island was an important point, making invasion difficult over a strait with notorious currents. So the history of early times is comparatively uneventful. This is shown by the merging of the Bronze Age civilization with that of the pre-ceding Stone Age, the evidence being the elaborate develop-ment of the cromlech burial. We see many cromlechs in Angle-sey, and can photograph them. Whenever we see Gothic type on our map we stop and investigate. There will always be something of interest to see.

Our party was interested in some of the discoveries made on the island. We found traces of primitive dwellings like clusters of hut circles. On Holyhead Mountain the work of excavation proved that dwellings here at any rate belonged to a time when metals were known and worked in the island. Other dwellings were underground or partly underground, supported even by vertical or horizontal poles, with turf roofs. (Very similar dwellings have been used by other primitive peoples in other parts of the world, especially in Alaska.) There have been signs of tents made with skins as well. Think of this when *your* tent is

M

pitched on some Anglesey farm and then realize why Anglesey is a land of legend and folk-lore.

The prehistoric remains, hut circles and burial chambers give the island a unique character which lends an atmosphere of mystery to the tour itself. Anglesey folk tell us entertaining tales of witchcraft and ghosts, of smuggling and wrecked ships. (We may even find golden sovereigns on Moelfre beach! The *Royal Charter*, a ship carrying more than £300,000 in gold, *en route* from Melbourne to Liverpool, went down close to the beach in the great storm of 1859.)

There must have been great thought for the dead judging by the extent and numbers of cromlechs existing. The Anglesey cromlechs invariably show abnormal features such as extra stone supports and chambers. The mode of construction by which great stone slabs were elevated without machinery is in itself remarkable. It is thought that possibly the building or monument in the course of erection was buried in a great mound of dry earth with an easy slope up which large stones could be dragged by main force.

Anglesey was famous for many things—as the last stronghold of the Druids; as a corn-growing country which could even supply all Wales; as the bulwark of the warrior princes of North Wales with a royal Palace at Aberffraw (there is a trace of it left there). As you look out over the Irish Sea from your tent doorways you can think of fearless Scandinavian sea-robbers who raided the island regularly. There are traces of this in many names in Anglesey and the Lleyn Peninsula. The name "Anglesey" itself may be from the Norse word *onguil* meaning a ford, and *ey* meaning an island. Thus "Ongullsey"—literally, an island by a ford or strait—would be possible. I often think what tremendous battles may have taken place on the shores of Anglesey when those sea-raiders landed from Scandinavia.

The Menai Straits delight everyone, especially yachtsmen. Tacitus records that the Romans crossed the Straits into Anglesey in A.D. 61. The crossing might have been much easier then, for at low tide the waters are believed to have been shallower than now. Agricola marched from the island to northern

England eighteen years later and made regular contact with Segontinum—known to us now as Caernarvon.

Other early settlers in Anglesey include the Irish. When we tour Holy Island we note the small inlets and bays called *porthau* on our map. These would be excellent landing places for small boats in good weather. We see the *Cytiau'r Gwyddelod* marked clearly—"the Irishmen's landing place".

We could also have a look at Beaumaris in detail. It has a French name, dating back to Edward the First. But for centuries it was a first-class port called Gwygr. It was one of the three privileged ports of Early Britain, the others being Newport (Monmouthshire) and Gwyddno (Cardigan Bay). In the past there was the important industry of copper-mining at Amlwch. We can see plenty of traces of that. It seems astonishing today to realize that less than 200 years ago Anglesey controlled the European copper market. No less than some 60,000–80,000 tons of ore were mined annually at Amlwch, yielding between 3,000 and 4,000 tons of copper. But there was no coal in Anglesey. So the ore had to be sent for smelting to Neath, Swansea and Lancashire. Amlwch developed from a tiny village to a thriving market town. Today it is the point where Atlantic liners, outward-bound from Liverpool, drop their pilots.

The Amlwch copper industry slumped when better deposits were found in Spain, but as late as 1914–18 copper precipitate was obtained by pumping methods. We can find some good subjects for our camera when trekking in this area.

We hear a great deal of Welsh spoken in Anglesey, for it is a stronghold of the Welsh language and culture. Some of the old Welsh people who know no English will talk in Welsh to the wandering Breton onion-sellers who go round the farms in late summer. They will answer back in their own dialect of Brittany and both understand each other. There are connections in many ways between these Celtic peninsulas of Brittany, Cornwall, Pembrokeshire and the Lleyn Peninsula and Anglesey.

J. H. Ingram, in his excellent book *The Islands of England*, says: "In Anglesey there is a feeling of age, of great age. If you have any feeling of the past you must be conscious of it . . .

it was long a land of mystery. Not for nothing was Anglesey known as 'the Dark Island'."

*　　　*　　　*

If we tackle a compact geographical area on these lines we shall soon be able to start an archaeological camp with confidence. There are not, relatively speaking, many opportunities of trekking because a good "dig" will take place at one special place, and we shall probably prefer to erect lightweight tents at the nearest good camp site and hope we can be of use when wanted.

Archaeologists, like detectives, search for clues from which sound deductions can be made. We can help them on "digs" by doing exactly what we are told, and by destroying nothing and moving nothing until the right moment. This attitude of mind and approach is most important for young people, if they want to see something for their endeavours, say a piece of Roman pottery carefully reassembled.

"Digs" are slow jobs because every bucket of soil has to be searched so carefully. The archaeologist in charge is not looking for gold coins or jewellery, although treasure might well turn up! *Where* he finds something is just as important as *what* it is he actually finds. An archaeologist says, in effect: wherever men have built or buried or even pitched their tents they have left behind articles which the passing of centuries does not destroy. The remains of a wooden post may be completely rotted but the earth will show where it stood. The kitchen refuse heap, thousands of years old, yields a rich harvest of evidence of what men ate and shows how they lived. A builder may accidentally drop a coin and "date" a whole series of objects for the archaeologist excavating centuries later. The position of objects in a site that was occupied for centuries may tell of conquests and great fires.

That is the *thrill* of archaeology which we can instil in young people. But besides this practical work we must remember the aids of modern science—the value of air photography and how it is used to indicate the sites of ancient settlements and dwellings, and the use of such remarkable inventions as the X-ray spectrometer and electronic computing device at Oxford which discovered the Piltdown hoax.

★ ★ ★

In most counties there is an archaeological society and full information regarding local digs in the summer will be well known to them. The youth leader in Britain can write to the Secretary of the Council for British Archaeology at 4 St. Andrew's Place, London, N.W.1.

The Council is able to give considerable help to youth groups wishing to help in archaeological field work. Each year, between March and September, a monthly list of sites upon which volunteers are required is circulated to subscribers for an annual fee of 10s. This *Calendar of Excavations* also contains references to special training schools.

In general, archaeological fieldwork is not suitable for young people under 16 because untrained workers have not got the right approach to the problem in hand, nor can they appreciate the need for care. Often the manual work is too heavy for them.

It is important to interpret archaeology to young people in its wider sense and not simply identify it with excavations, exciting as these always are to boys and girls. Young people can do much useful work on field surveys if a suitable leader is available and reference should certainly be made to E. S. Wood's *Collins Field Guide*. Help is also needed in the field of industrial archaeology and the *Handbook for Industrial Archaeologists* by Kenneth Hudson provides useful guidance.

It is sometimes possible for small groups of boys and girls, accompanied by, say, a master, to take part in a "dig" but much depends on the existence of a suitable site. By "suitable" I mean one on which the problems are to some extent known in advance, the area to be examined is sufficiently large to accommodate a number of untrained workers, and the soil is of a kind to enable beginners to notice changes in stratification.

These points are worth noting because otherwise it might be thought that parties of volunteers could be accepted on all sites. In practice individuals, or small parties of twos or threes, may stand a better chance of being accepted as helpers than a large party. An enthusiastic, willing intelligent boy of 17 would only be refused as a helper on a dig if enough helpers were already available, or work of a special character was in progress.

Parties which wish to try and gain some experience on the Continent may care to write to the Association for Cultural Exchange, 8–10 High Street, Haverhill, Suffolk, and ask for a copy of the booklet *Opportunities to Excavate Abroad*. This may well provide opportunities for the individual or a small party to gain first-class experience. The Association seeks "dedicated amateurs under the age of 35" for such work.

Young people often think that digs are the only things that archaeologists do. *In fact the real work is in examining in detail the results of the dig.* Every modern science is now used, and I have had the opportunity of seeing this at first hand in progress at the Institute of Archaeology at London University.

Modern science has revolutionized prehistory. For instance, the radioactivity of wood, hair, bones and organic matter can be measured in scientific terms to determine when it was formed. A small piece of charcoal from a pit at Stonehenge suggested to scientists, using the measurement of radioactivity as a guide, that the oak from which it was made was alive and growing some 3,800 years ago. But such samples must be taken by trained field workers to have any scientific value.

*   *   *

To show what is possible let me recall that senior boys from a Bury school, under the guidance of a skilled archaeologist, uncovered a Bronze Age skeleton, while others in Yorkshire helped in the excavation of a Roman-British cemetery at York. In this case they did the usual carting and hoisting, and also cleared bones and pottery on the site.

The 1968 Calendar of Excavations of the Council for British Archaeology included these projects:

1. *East Bight, Lincoln.* Twelve volunteers were needed at a time to help in excavations to determine the position of the Eastern defences at the legionary fortress.

2. *Matson Camp, near Gloucester.* Preliminary excavations on

a small scale on a site believed to be Early Iron Age. Volunteers were needed.

3. *Acton Burnell, Shropshire.* Volunteers were required for Sunday duties on the site of the Roman road and bridge under excavation.

4. *Cricklade, Gloucestershire.* Volunteers were welcomed at the excavation of the ancient town "walls", special interest being attached to the role of Cricklade in Anglo-Saxon times.

5. *William's Hill, Middleham, North Riding, Yorkshire.* About twelve volunteers and a photographer were needed to help in work on a motte and bailey earthwork in Wensleydale built about 1086 and replaced by a stone castle about 1170. Beginners were trained to help.

6. *Northolt, Middlesex.* Weekend excavation took place on a twelfth- to seventeenth-century moated site. Camping was encouraged and volunteers were welcomed.

7. *Tan y Bwlch, Aberystwyth.* About ten volunteers were needed on work at a Norman motte and bailey castle. Beginners were accepted and trained, and camping was possible.

8. *St. Mary's Abbey, Yorkshire.* Beginners were accepted and trained for voluntary work on Roman and medieval levels.

*   *   *

The Council for British Archaeology co-ordinates such work in Britain, usually through the County or local Archaeological Society. It should not be confused with the Institute of Archaeology at London University, which was opened in 1937 as a centre of academic research for training in the professional field. The institute provides a two years' full-time, or three years' part-time, course of study reading to a post-graduate diploma in archaeology for those who have already taken a Bachelor of Arts degree. It is thus a training centre for professional archaeologists, most of whom work in museums, and is quite unsuitable for young people. The address is: The Secretary, Institute of Archaeology, University of London, 31–34 Gordon Square, London, W.C.1.

For most practical purposes the Secretary of the Council for

British Archaeology will be more likely to help youth leaders seeking tasks for a small trekking party keen on archaeology.

FURTHER READING

Teach Yourself Geology—Dr. A. Raistrick (English Universities Press)

Teach Yourself Archaeology—S. Graham Brade-Birks (English Universities Press)

Prehistoric Britain—J. and C. Hawkes (Chatto & Windus)

Field Guide to Archaeology—Eric S. Wood (Collins)

Man the Toolmaker—K. P. Oakley (British Museum of Natural History)

The Weald—S. W. Wooldridge and Frederick Goldring (Collins)

Ancient Monuments of Anglesey—O. E. Craster (H.M.S.O., 1965)

Archaeology from A to Z—G. Palmer and N. Lloyd (Warne). A detailed dictionary of archaeology with special reference to terms used, sites in the British Isles and museums. It is incomplete, however, though first published in 1968, and the reader is advised to add his or her own notes pending further editions.

CHAPTER 16

Map Making

THE first serious map I ever made was accomplished on foot by compass traverse in Dovedale, with Hartington Youth Hostel as a base. At other times I have lived in a lightweight tent for as much as four months at a time, making a plane table survey on a scale of 1 : 25,000 of a large area of North and Central Wales. The possibilities are endless, and if my own academic and military training as a geographer and field surveyor has given me a special enthusiasm for map making, I hope I shall not stress it unduly. There are so many activities to try outdoors when camping or hostelling, and map making is only one of them. But it *is* an important activity, especially suited to the capacities and enthusiasm of young people on trek.

There is simply not the space in a book like this to go into the theory and practice of field survey in detail; the aim rather is to give teachers, youth leaders and all young people ideas to try out for themselves, in an attempt to widen their horizons and given them better standards of achievement on outdoor treks.

I shall assume therefore that map reading has been mastered, that a compass can be used properly and that the reader is already acquainted with the usual map terms, such as triangulation scale, height, conventional signs, representative fraction, bearing, horizontal equivalent and so on. (There are some excellent books available on the background of mapping and local surveys; see the Further Reading list.)

Geography is a practical outdoor subject if done properly, and young people have probably already tackled such familiar problems as making plans of the school playing-fields or the local public park, keeping field note-books of chained distances and offsets in a neat and methodical fashion so that draughtsmen could work from such notes if necessary.

We must look for work with more scope if we are going to map on trek. I would suggest that the party first masters the measuring of *direction*. This will entail a good deal of practice in taking compass bearings and differentiating clearly between magnetic, true and back bearings. Young people have to learn that a bearing indicates the angle between North and the object being observed, measured from North and always in a clockwise direction. It is never necessary to say more than "the bearing of the electricity pylon is 250°", for instance. The direction from true North is the true bearing, but if we are using a magnetic compass the direction it indicates will be a magnetic bearing.

We must therefore allow for the magnetic variation between true and magnetic bearing, and not confuse the two. A back bearing is frequently confused. It is nothing more than the bearing the observer's actual position would have if someone else were measuring it from the distant object. Thus a back bearing on a selected object must differ from its bearing by 180°. The bearing on our electricity pylon might be 250° due West, but the observer there would see us at 70° due East. The back bearing of the pylon would be 70°.

*   *   *

We must master the use of the Chain and prismatic compass first because we shall do some chain surveying and traversing before going on to plane table work. The surveying chain, or "Gunter's Chain", is 22 yards long, with 100 steel links and two handles at either end. Thus 100 links=1 chain; 10 chains =1 furlong, and 8 furlongs=1 mile. (For longer distances a 100-feet chain is used but we shall stick to our short chain.)

The Prismatic Compass is an accurate card compass with the great advantage that the observer can see the reading he requires at the same time as he carries out the observation, and what is more it is the correct bearing since it is from the outer

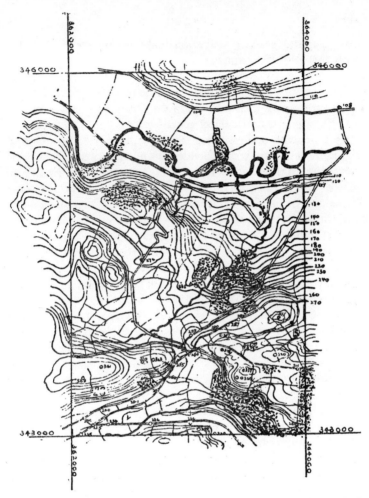

Section of original map made by the author, using plane table methods on a scale of 1 : 25,000, of part of the Tanat Valley, Central Wales. The survey was undertaken with a party of thirty-two experienced senior boys, average age 17½, working in pairs on the adjoining sixteen sections. All the edges were compared closely and checked independently. The party used lightweight camp kit and a central base camp; plane tablers were taken out to their sections each morning by car. All the work was done under field conditions in June and completed in ten days

ring. Regular practice will soon make young people familiar with this splendid compass.

Traversing. We can now make simple maps in "green" country by traversing methods, using the chain, prismatic compass and pacing. It is particularly good for following a well-defined stream or river, and mapping its course, or a hill track. One of the authors of the recommended book, *Maps*, recalls how he carried out a traverse in Africa along a winding marshy stream which could only be approached by canoe! He therefore "counted the number of paddle strokes along a measured bank, and found that each stroke of the paddlers sent the canoe along $4\frac{1}{2}$ feet". He then counted the number of paddle strokes made in a given time, so that when passing over long distances he would know, from the total time taken, the approximate number of paddle strokes, each taking the canoe along $4\frac{1}{2}$ feet, that had been made from start to finish.

At the end of a twenty-seven mile traverse, during which a small boy was detailed to beat a gong to keep the paddling uniform, he found the error was less than 3 per cent. Personally I feel he should have been knighted.

A closed traverse is one which ends (at least in theory!) where it began. The open traverse is the one we shall use most of all on trek. It cannot be self-checking, like a closed traverse, but we can check its accuracy in other ways. We can, for instance, find the correct bearing and distance of the finishing point on our O.S. map and plot it on our own plan. The distance between our finishing point and that one is the error of closure, and the aim is to get it as small as possible. (As far as young people are concerned this method will suffice for the time being. They can learn two other methods later when they have more confidence and experience.)

The leader can, at his discretion, go into traversing in more detail showing how to adjust errors of closure, how to plot a point by intersection or resection from known positions, and how to "sketch-in" field detail rapidly and accurately on his traverse as he goes along. It needs careful and skilled adult supervision, and it can be great fun, based on youth hostels or tents. Everything depends on the abilities and experience of the young people in the party and it is wise *not to attempt too much at any one time*. In practice I have found it useful to send teams of two or three senior boys out on traverse on their own from a tented base, say, using compass and pacing and making up their own field books. This is preferable to the usual traversing by party in which a few enthusiasts do the real work, while the rest amble along and watch.

Plane Tabling. The teacher or experienced youth leader who can find time to run a plane table survey of a selected area will find it of the greatest value to young people. It brings so many qualities to bear on the single problem of mapping a region which, for all practical purposes, can *always* be "unknown and unexplored". To do this job properly we shall need skill and knowledge and patience for the actual field work. But to these we must add initiative, an eye for country, a breadth of vision and outlook, high standards of camping, polished team work, and an ability to keep going cheerfully if inclement weather sets in, as it will surely do in a British summer.

Plane tabling is considered somewhat out-of-date for serious mapping now. In World War II most of the Army maps used were made from air photos; field maps were revised by air survey methods—but in some cases the Allied advance was so rapid that actual air photos themselves had to be used. Skilled plane tabling still has its place in survey, and the actual work itself gives a degree of satisfaction and a quality of *absolute accuracy* in the field work which is unsurpassed by air survey.

My own method has been based entirely on field practice over a long period, in widely differing terrains both in Britain and overseas. We start by finding a selected training area for plane table mapping practice in pairs. This training area need not be at all large—a few square miles will suffice if it contains a reasonable variety of natural features. I find a useful training area for young people about the age of 16 to 20 can be bounded by a natural framework of railway lines, main or secondary roads, and a river or stream. Within the framework we look for undulating country, giving the party the chance to practise

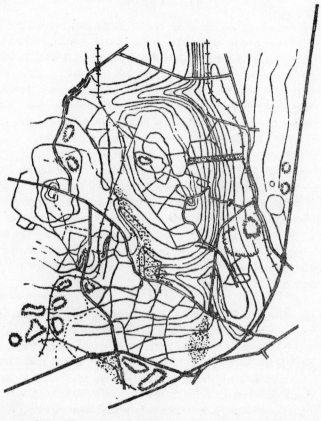

Map made by the author of a suitable training area for young people who wished to try map making under experienced adult supervision. It is a compact area, bounded conveniently by roads and railway, and containing "something of everything". The map features include some interesting contours; woodland; roads; field boundaries; colliery slag-heaps; some deep pools; a variety of railway track; and field paths. Similar areas may easily be found on 1 : 63,360 (one inch) or 1 : 25,000 O.S. maps and then used as a local training area on any required scale

contouring, plotting natural features and landmarks, roads, railways, streams, lakes or ponds, buildings, farms and so on. The mapping of this training area should be done on the same scale as the open country to be tackled later. For all practical purposes in Britain a scale of 1 : 25,000 (2½ in. to the mile, approximately) will be found most effective for simple plane tabling.

No youngster should proceed from the training area until he or she has mastered the elementary principles of plane tabling and made a fair map of the area entirely by his or her own efforts and draughtsmanship. In practice serious plane tabling is done alone. The surveyors are taken out to their own areas by transport and then left alone to work on their plane tables until sundown, when transport returns to collect them. The plane tabler, of course, works from "trig points" (trigonometrical stations) already established in the triangulated territory. His job becomes one of filling in the detail and for all practical purposes this can be its main use with field parties of young people.

We can divide our proposed area into convenient sections and then plot accurately the positions of all "trig stations" within each section. The field work within each section can then start from a convenient "trig station".

Few youngsters are likely to have enough experience to do their own plane table work in detail alone. I would suggest parties of two or three to one plane table, sharing the work and the load. If a youth hostel is used as a base the equipment can be taken there by transport, but in the case of a lightweight camp the use of a barn or outbuilding should be arranged at the farm. The gear and equipment can then be sent there by road or rail, and kept there; in addition the building can be used as a drawing office for doing the "inking in" on wet or misty days, and so on. The trek then becomes a series of daily sorties in small parties from a tented rendezvous, with the use of a barn or outbuilding for drawing and "wet day" work. This kind of trek is different from anything else we have advocated in this book, and it is suggested now because of the physical limitations of the young people likely to be tackling plane tabling.

If some senior boys of intelligence and stamina wish to trek, carrying plane table equipment and lightweight camp kit, let them do so, again in small parties of two or three with kit pruned to a minimum and shared equally. It can be a very strenuous and exacting job at any time of the year, but it has been done successfully by the British Schools Exploring Society. The leader will simply have to guage the capabilities of his party and work accordingly. Some kind of initial transport, e.g. Land-Rover or 15-cwt. lorry, is essential for taking the party and kit to the chosen area.

*   *   *

The success of the plane tabler depends largely on the accuracy of the trigonometrical control, and this means careful choice of terrain. A good plane tabler likes to interpolate from "trig" points once or twice a day at least, and in practice possibly every hour. He should not have to carry clinometer heights further than three miles from a "trig" height. I was taught that the density of "trig" points must always be fixed by distances and visibility and that it is quite independent of the scale on which the map is being made. A plane tabler renowned in the Royal Engineers said: "As a very practical point the trig-observer must remember that the plane tabler has no telescope on his alidade. He must therefore choose objects with enough bulk to stand up clearly to the eyes. A cairn on a hill is worth a dozen poles. A wind pump is useless if surrounded by a dozen like itself. Trig heights should be provided in valleys as well as on hill-tops." We can see the force of that observation when we are on a plane table trek in the hills.

The following points need emphasis as far as young people working from camp or youth hostels are concerned:

1. The smaller-size plane table may be more convenient in use. (The sizes vary from 15 in. by 15 in. to 18 in. by 24 in.) Ensure that some kind of cover is carried for wet weather protection.

2. From the very start let the survey proceed properly with the best quality linen-backed cartridge paper used on the table and placed firmly on the board with edges of 2 in. or

3 in. folded round and pasted correctly, to give a perfectly smooth, flat, wrinkle-free, writing surface without any tightness or distortion.

3. Insist on high standards of neatness, accuracy and draughtsmanship. The initial grid placed on the plane table must be drawn with graphic accuracy and all relevant "trig" points fixed accurately, with co-ordinates double-checked.

4. Kit must be kept clean and in good order at all times, and especially if borrowed. Plane tables can easily be knocked over or ruined by a curious heifer. Watch out for local animals, and trust none of them! Also watch where one's own feet are placed.

5. A plane-tabler's basic kit would consist of plane table and cover; trough compass; Indian clinometer (for heights and contouring); alidade or sighting rule; box scales of the correct scale for the survey; protractor; straight edges; a good supply of first quality 2H, 3H, 4H pencils with soft eraser, razor blades, and sharp penknife all in suitable box; crowquill or "ladies" pens with a good supply of first quality waterproof Indian and coloured inks (Higgins' inks are excellent). But make allowances for individual preferences and do not overstress what a basic kit should be, or the arguments will last for days, and even weeks! Carry a supply of stout rubber bands to place round all loose items to prevent rattle when carried.

6. The plane tabler must show clearly the ground he has surveyed and mapped. He is drawing for explanation rather than reproduction. What is wanted is a fair but accurate map of the area, not an artistic sketch which may be hopelessly inaccurate from a survey point of view. But a plane tabler must be a neat hand at pencil work and Indian ink penning-in.

7. Do each piece of work systematically in pencil on the plane table before inking-in. Avoid unnecessary rays. "Today's work is to-morrow's control", is a good maxim. A good memory is a tremendous asset in assessing topography (remembering what was behind that high copse when we went there four days ago, for instance).

N

8. Take every advantage of fine weather. Excellent survey work can be done both in early morning and evening in fine, summer weather.
9. Each pair or trio of plane tablers will have adjoining areas to survey. Edges must therefore be compared regularly, and accurately, to make the finished map a worthy one. My own map of the Tanat Valley on page 187 was one section in a total territory of sixteen adjoining sections.
10. Once the vertical interval for contours has been established stick to it rigidly for all sections of the area. On a scale of 1 : 25,000 a good V.I. is fifty feet in hilly country, or say ten metres if we are working in metric measure.

Useful adjuncts to the trekking party going map making are: Plastic transparent, flat *map cases* with zip fasteners; *map measure and curvimeter* for tracing a plan of the route to be measured against the map or plan scale; *map measurer* for using with maps of all scales (the pointer wheel is run over the map route and the distance read off in the aperture); *pedometer* for recording accurately the distances trekked (a multi-position regulator enables the user to adjust the instrument to his or her own stride).

FURTHER READING

Maps—Alexander D'Agapeyeff and E. C. R. Hadfield (Oxford University Press)
Map Making—Frank Debenham (Cambridge University Press)
Army Manual of Map Reading and Field Survey—(H.M.S.O.)
Textbook of Topographical Surveying—C. F. Close (H.M.S.O.)
Making Local Surveys: An Eye for Country—Charlotte A. Simpson (Pitman)
Geography from the Air—F. Walker (Methuen)
The Lost Villages of England—Maurice Beresford (Lutterworth Press)

INDEX

Index